Marcia Brenner.
from
Katharine Wright
X-mas 1980

DOLLS IN COLOR

Dolls in Color

FAITH EATON

Photography Bob Loosemore

Macmillan Publishing Co., Inc.
New York

Macmillan Publishing Co., Inc.
866 Third Avenue, New York, N.Y. 10022

Library of Congress Cataloging in Publication Data

Eaton, Faith.
  Dolls in color.

  (Macmillan color series)
  Bibliography: p.
  Includes index.
  1. Dolls. I. Title. II. Series.
NK4893.F25   1976   745·59′22   75-17668
ISBN 0-02-534710-1

First American Edition 1976

Color printed in Great Britain by Colour Reproductions, Billericay
Text printed and books bound by Tinling (1973) Ltd, Merseyside

Contents

Acknowledgments

The author is indebted to many people for their kind help during the book's production: those who have generously allowed dolls from their collection to be photographed, those who have given of their time and shared their knowledge, and, above all, those who have patiently allowed me to put aside tasks of equal importance in order that this one might be completed first.

Particularly appreciative thanks are offered to: Jim Fordham, Caroline Goodfellow and the Staff of the Bethnal Green Museum; Mr and Mrs Maitland of Holly Trees Museum, Colchester, Essex; Josephine Conrad-Wissa, Jackie Jacobs and Mary Johnson. Sincere thanks are also due to: the Director and Staff of the Horniman Museum, Dulwich; the RSPCA Museum, Haulith House, Cheddar, Somerset; the director of the Holly Trees Museum, Colchester, Celia Chambers; Angela Houghton; G. E. Russell and J. Whyberd. Also to Mrs B. Woollacott for her helpful information about her mother's family, the Pierottis.

Without the co-operation of Bob Loosemore the book could not have been produced; he is gratefully thanked for his exemplary patience as well as his excellent photographs. Thanks are also due to Mrs R. Kloegman, who deciphered and typed the manuscript and thereby enabled it to be published.

The dolls in the following plates appear by kind permission of their owners or trustees: 4, 52, 53, 62, 63, and the pincushion doll in plate 66, Holly Trees Museum; 67 and 79, Bethnal Green Museum; 75 *left* and 75 *right*, the Horniman Museum; 64 the RSPCA's Collection at Cheddar; 6, 7, 25, 36, 41, 42, 43, 44, 46, 47, 48 above and the 'Bye-lo Baby' in plate 31, Jackie Jacobs; the 'Little Fanny' doll in plate 15, Celia Chambers; 8, Angela Houghton; 67, Mary Johnson; 5 by G. E. Russell; 77 by J. Whyberd. All other dolls appearing in the book are from the author's own collection.

Preface

Just as people of different nationalities emigrate and settle in other countries, adopting some of the new homeland's customs yet retaining many of their old, so dolls have been taken from place to place, and altered and adapted according to need. This tends to make a nonsense of any strict dividing line between 'Display' and 'Play' dolls; as circumstances and environments change, so does the usage of the doll. Learned men are still undecided as to whether many of the 'dolls' found in ancient tombs were actually playthings, or fetishes, idols, substitute human sacrifices, talismen and so on.

And so the doll historian is faced with two problems from the beginning: not only to wonder whether the object under review is really a doll at all, in the generally accepted sense of the word, but then to ponder – should it be classified as a decorative and/or instructional ornament, or as a children's plaything?

The answer, as usual, must be a compromise. For the sake of convenience a guide-line, rather than a dividing line, has sorted the dolls in this book into different categories. But it must be acknowledged that the line is both tenuous and flexible; one child's toy may be another child's idol. A 'fashion doll' may have been a necessity to a dress-maker, a whim to a wealthy woman; and, depending on family circumstances, either a plaything or a strictly ornamental heirloom to a child.

Certain countries had world-wide reputations for dollmaking: Japan, with two utterly different styles of traditional dolls; France, to which all the world looked for its fashion dolls, expensive creations

7

for children and 'toys' for adults; the Tyrol, with Holland's aid, providing cheap little wooden playthings; England, renowned for its heavy wooden and flimsy paper dolls, its intriguing pedlars and beautiful wax dolls; the USA with all its regional folk dolls and clever commercial inventions; Germany, world famous for porcelain and bisque, wax and wooden headed dolls; these are only some of the 'giants' in the saga of dollmaking. Believing that the dolls of ancient Rome, Greece and Egypt have, by comparison, a limited appeal, they have not been included in this book; which in the main spans the period between the sixteenth and twentieth centuries.

As the many pages of colour photographs form such an important part of the book, the subjects have been most carefully chosen to illustrate the theme of the story of dollmaking. Obviously, for any book smaller than a weighty encyclopedia, there has to be some drastic pruning of certain branches. However, the aim always, in making this very personal choice of dolls, has been to choose examples which will not only adorn, but illuminate, the main outline of their prolific family tree.

I

Dolls on Display

Throughout the world many of the dolls made for display also had a religious or instructional function to perform. The Japanese Festival Dolls are supreme examples of this type of dual-purpose doll. So, on a different level, are the Russian 'nest' dolls, since they are both ornaments and real playthings. Somewhere between these two extremes stand the English Pedlars and Fortune Tellers, and the Japanese 'shelf' dolls.

Japanese dolls once had a caste-system as rigid and complex as any designed for human beings. But, in keeping with the times perhaps, over the years some barriers have disappeared and the dividing line between 'Play' and 'Display' dolls is difficult to discern.

Perhaps the best known of the truly decorative Japanese display dolls are the *sakura-ningyō* (literally, cherry doll), often made to represent Kabuki dancers and characters. These dolls are made commercially and frequently exported, they are also the kind made by Japanese amateur dollmakers. Dollmaking is extremely popular in Japan as a hobby, rivalling the art of flower arranging, and there are schools which exist solely to provide instruction in dollmaking. In a Japanese home the sakura-ningyō is placed on a shelf, usually in an alcove in the living room, where it may be regarded as a pleasing, ornamental conversion-piece; see plate 1.

Also used for decoration nowadays are the ubiquitous *kokeshi*, little wooden dolls resembling nine-pins. But, as will be mentioned, the origins and insertions of Japanese dolls are nothing if not complicated, and the story of kokeshi is more properly told in the play-doll section; see plate 10.

9

The exquisite *hina-ningyō* (Festival dolls), plate 2, could never be confused with mundane playthings. For well over four hundred years these delicately fashioned dolls, their faces often coated with layers of gofun (pulverized oyster shells and glue), polished to the shining quality of ivory, and costumed in rich brocades and silk, have been the heirlooms of the wealthy. Poorer families set up their festival displays with clay or papier mâché dolls dressed in coloured paper or just painted.

The ancestors of all hina-ningyō were made entirely of paper. Old Chinese beliefs and Japanese Shinto ideas about purification combined some thousand years ago and led to the use of paper 'talismen' in certain rites on special feast days, when little paper dolls were cast into the river to bear away the thrower's sins. Gradually the custom changed. Instead of destroying paper dolls, the practice of displaying beautiful, more elaborate dolls, reflecting Japanese life and traditions, changed the nature of these festivals. Later, during the Edo period (1614–1868), accessories as well as dolls were formally displayed on tiered stands.

The twentieth century has brought many changes to Japan, and westernisation has diminished the respected symbolism of the displays on the two remaining Festival days. That of *Ohina-matsuri* (literally, Honourable Small Dolls' Festival), more generally known as the Girls' Festival, begins on the third day of the third month, that is 3 March in the western calendar. *Tango-no-sekku* (literally, The First Horse-day of the Festival – or, more colloquially, The Red-letter day) is the Boys' Festival and takes place on the fifth day of the fifth month, that is 5 May.

Of the two, the Girls' Festival became the more elaborate and important, for it was through the arrangement of the dolls, and the entertaining involved, that mothers taught their daughters their duties and obligations, the family's and the nation's customs, and the importance of maintaining traditional Japanese culture. Some days before the actual festival a room, or alcove, in the house is cleaned and prepared. A stand, covered with a red cloth, is set up and the boxes of hina-ningyō are brought out of storage and the dolls unpacked. They are only taken out of their boxes for the duration of the festival, for the rest of the year they are safely packed away. These dolls are treasured heirlooms, passed from mother to eldest daughter when she, as a bride, goes to her new home. Younger daughters have sets of hina-ningyō collected for them by relatives, who present them to the child before the first festival day following their birth.

There are two traditional ways of setting up the display, according to whether the family had noble or military connections, and if they followed the pattern maintained in Kyōto or Yedo – the former being the simpler arrangement.

Those following the Yedo tradition would have a five- or seven-tiered stand and arrange the dolls thus:

Top tier: Two *Dairi-bina* (dolls representing the Emperor and Empress)
Second tier: Three *kwanjo* (maids of honour)
Third tier: Five *gonin-bayashi* (court musicians)
Fourth tier: Two *zuijin* (Imperial guards)
Fifth tier: Three *shichō* (equerries)

On the lowest tiers, the sixth and seventh, would be placed sets of miniature lacquer household furnishings and personal possessions, which represent the dowry a nobleman's daughter would have as a bride. They are often, in their own right, perfect little works of art.

In former times aristocratic brides rode to their new homes in ox-carts, and those from military families were carried in palanquins. So, according to the family's associations or preference, a miniature lacquer ox-cart or a palanquin would be added to the display.

In some wealthy families more court dolls were added to the lower shelves and the whole display set before a miniature building representing a palace, but this was never a general rule.

All displays would, in addition to the dolls, have the miniature cherry tree and orange tree representing the two growing in the palace courtyard at Kyōto. And, in some homes, a delicately painted screen, two lanterns and two miniature dogs – symbols of loyalty – would protect the elevated Dairi-bina throughout the Festival.

As the mother handed each item to her daughter, to place on the appropriate tier, she would explain its significance; and so, surely in the nicest possible way, the little girl would learn the hierarchy of the Court, the virtues of obedience and loyalty, the duties of a wife and the importance of Japanese culture.

On the day of the Festival miniature diamond shaped rice cakes (*hishi-mochi*) and a kind of sweetened saké (*shiro-zaké*) were added to the lowest tier. Later these would be offered, first to the Dairi-bina, and then to the more appreciative relatives and friends calling in to celebrate the special day and admire the display.

The Boys' Festival evolved from the Edo Samurai custom of making a little display outside their houses on the Festival of Shōbu (the Iris), which fell on 5 May. The warrior's *nobori* (a war-banner some 3 m (10 ft) in length) flew from its bamboo pole, and carp streamers decorated the stand on which he placed his helmet, spear and halberd. Eventually the displays became so elaborate and costly that they were restricted by law. Instead, it became customary to display miniature figures and weapons indoors, leaving only the carp streamers, symbols of courageous energy, fluttering from their bamboo poles outside; see plate 3.

Gradually 5 May became the day on which families celebrated the birth of their sons. And then, finally, this indoor miniature display was designated as the Boys' Festival Day. One cannot help feeling that perhaps the celebration was partly adopted in order to encourage traditional manly virtues, and partly in order to pacify small boys, furious at being left out of the Ohina-matsuri festivities.

The stand for Tango-no-Sekku has two or three tiers, and is covered in green material. As for Ohina-matsuri, there are two ways of arranging exhibits on it. One had the miniature replicas of pieces of armour in the centre, with dolls and models of folk heroes and samurai each side, and model war-horse, fans and drums towards the front. The other arrangement placed the dolls in the centre, with all the accoutrements around them. Both displays had, towards the rear of the stand, miniature banners and standards, backed by a curtain which was a small replica of those used in battle camps.

Originally *shōbu-saké* and *mochi* (rice-cakes) were prepared, placed in front of the display, and offered to guests. Later it became customary to place imitation mochi on the stand for display only although it is interesting to note that the shōbu-saké still retained its refreshing quality.

The Japanese love of symbolism and their traditional ancestor worship is well demonstrated on the Boys' Festival. About a thousand years ago the iris, closely associated with warriors owing to its sword-like leaves, was dedicated on the third day of the fifth month. The next day was devoted to decorating the place and, on 5 May, the Emperor watched special displays of sword-play and archery. As all Japanese boys were once taught that 'the sword is the soul of the Samurai', it is easy to see why the Iris plays a part in the Festival. It is also regarded as a charm against illness and evil spirits, so is indeed an appropriate flower for a child.

The name of this Festival, 'The First Horse-Day', refers to its probable Chinese origin. There, 5 May was a day devoted to horse-racing and competitive games, and it is believed that the Japanese ceremony evolved from this source.

There are some interesting dollmaking parallels in the islands of Japan and Britain. Referring only to the display dolls made in Japan and England, miniature replicas of well-known characters were made for ornamental purposes in the home in both countries, and many of the dolls were also instructional; although the styles differ greatly, professional dollmakers in both countries used local woods to make fine, expensive dolls and the cheapest little playthings; and, amateur dollmaking and dressing are hobbies which still flourish in both countries.

Statues and figurines decorate homes all over the world; but, although the defining line between figurines and dolls is often anything but clear, it does seem that only in England and Japan were 'proper' dolls used mainly, if not solely, as ornaments. But, whereas the Japanese lady loved to have a delicate model of a graceful dancer in her room, the Victorian English lady – and how typically English this is – elevated to her drawing-room a miniature replica of a very different character. For the most famous of all English display dolls is surely the red-cloaked Pedlar doll; see plate 4.

As pedlars were once such a welcome and familiar sight in so many countries, it does seem curious that only in England were Pedlar

13

dolls made and appreciated. Figurines of street-vendors of all kinds, of course, have been made all over the world, but the traditionally dressed Pedlar dolls seem to have been an English speciality. Although there are some indigenous red-cloaked 'Notion Nanny' dolls in the USA, they are comparatively modern and, usually, playdolls.

During Victoria's long reign the idea of a 'conversation piece' used as a drawing-room ornament became increasingly popular, and the Pedlar doll under its glass cover was thought particularly suitable for a prominent position on many an overmantle or what-not. Tenniel's illustrations of 'Alice' climbing through the looking-glass show two such shades, protecting a vase and clock on the mantle-piece; one longs to know if an unseen third covered another vase or a Pedlar doll.

Most Pedlar dolls were made as old women, wearing red or russet hooded cloaks, black bonnets over white caps, and white aprons over print dresses, although occasionally a pretty girl Pedlar was made; see plate 5. A few men dolls accompanied their female companions, and some of these were made to commemorate the granting of hawkers' licences to Crimean War veterans.

The accessories of the dolls also attracted attention; their trays or baskets of tiny wares made them peculiarly fascinating. If genuinely contemporaneous with the doll the wares often give clues to its date. For example, cotton *on wooden reels* must mean a post-1830's doll, as full-size ones were only invented for commercial use at the beginning of Victoria's reign. Tiny calendars and books are obviously useful, and so are certain prints. One depicting 'New London Bridge' can hardly have been placed in the basket when the doll was made if this was *before* the bridge's opening in 1831. But, as additional wares have so often been placed in the Pedlar dolls' baskets over the years, their contents alone cannot be relied upon to date the dolls unless it is absolutely certain they have not been altered.

At the height of their popularity, an adult could buy a Pedlar doll complete with wares; or else a doll with an empty basket and then have the pleasure of searching for small ivory or silver trinkets with which to fill it, a far more satisfactory way of displaying a little collection of miniatures than the usual row fringing a shelf-edge in the china cabinet. At the other end of the scale quite small children could be usefully occupied for hours – a necessity in those well-regulated days when idleness was a Sin – making minute samplers, pin-cushions, books, and dozens of other tiny items for the Pedlar's stock.

In some fortunate families indulgent adults might buy little papier mâché or peg-wooden dolls and dress them, perhaps as replicas of particular pedlars remembered from youth. If skilful enough, they might even make the dolls themselves. The long skirt and cloak would hide a stick-like body, and an old kid glove finger, with the help of the Victorian lady's ubiquitous box of water-colour paints, would provide a most adequate face.

From the early nineteenth century certain firms had specialised in making Pedlar dolls: C. and H. White of Portsmouth made kid-headed Pedlars, Evans and Cartwright of Wolverhampton used papier mâché, and produced dolls in a dozen different sizes, which indicates the demand. Throughout the century firms made Pedlar dolls of wax, wood, papier mâché; while in the country areas talented amateurs contrived theirs from anything handy, often using dried apples or nuts to produce suitably wrinkled old pedlar faces. But whether commercial or ·home-made, 'Maud Heath', 'Sarah Cutler', 'Sarah Thrifty', 'Sarah Trippins' (the popularity of that Christian name is interesting), stood under glass shades protected from all dust, and one wonders what their real life prototypes, tramping the filthy roads, would have thought of such protective care.

Although 'Polly Jones' carries her credentials, 'Licensed Hawker 109', pinned to her basket, strictly speaking only pedlars carried their wares; hawkers used pack mules, ponies or donkeys. Remarkably, few, if any, true hawkers seem to have attracted the dollmakers, but stall-holers and their produce, particularly during the second half of the nineteenth century, were made with both imagination and skill. The farm produce of one includes tubs of fruit and vegetables, sacks of nuts, and baskets of eggs and fowls. Another, also made *c.* 1890, concentrates so hard on the artistic presentation of her trays of fish and barrels of shell-fish that the very arrangement of the ribbons trimming her own bonnet resembles the seaweed decorating her stall.

It seems ironic that the Victorian lady, who probably never descended the basement stairs to speak to her kitchen staff, let alone a pedlar at the back door, should choose to give pride of place in her drawing-room to a Pedlar doll. No doubt the fascination of the miniature wares was the most likely cause of the appeal. One should not always assume, however, that the Victorians were completely devoid of a sense of humour; one enchanting young Victorian Pedlar doll has prominently displayed on her tray 'French love songs' and '*English* wedding-rings'.

There is also a more aristocratic version of the market-woman and her stall. The charity bazaar was a familiar feature of Victorian life, and some exquisite examples were made of booths and stalls with fashionably delicate silk-clad sellers and buyers.

Another composite conversation piece was the home-made room, containing a group of little dolls arranged in a scene. Whether the setting was a wedding reception in a drawing-room, a needlework session in a nursery or schoolroom, all the small inhabitants would be most carefully and suitably dressed and arranged before the room was placed in its glazed box or cabinet; see plate 6.

Far removed from these amateur productions were the expensive and fascinating French and German automata. Musicians and dancers played and danced, clowns and conjurors performed, animals and children amused, old women knitted or slept and young ones sighed and combed their hair. All delighted the onlooker with their beautiful costumes, and clever mechanical movements to the pleasing sound of a hidden musical box. Although famous makers had been producing automata since the early part of the eighteenth century, it was the decade of the 1780s which provided some of the most illustrious names: Vaucanson, Kintzing and Roentgen – who made the famous dulcimer player for Marie Antoinette – and the two Jacquet-Droz, the brilliant father and son who created the almost uncanny mechanical artists and writers.

Oddly enough, a century later, the 1880s also produced a spate of particularly skilful and famous makers of automata: Roullet and his son-in-law, Ernest Decamps, were among the best and the firm they founded is still making superb automata today; see plate 7.

There is an element of surprise in so many of these display dolls. Wind the key and the ornamental automaton suddenly performs to music from a hidden source; fold back the skirt of the Fortune Teller doll and carefully open one of the fragile 'pleats' of her multi-coloured paper petticoat – on it will be written your fate. Sometimes these dolls, who reached the height of their popularity in England in the mid to late nineteenth century, wore fabric skirts and petticoats. Into rows of small numbered pockets stitched round the hems were inserted tiny rolled-up paper 'fortunes'; see plate 8.

Another version was a combined Pedlar and Fortune Teller. A doll, usually a pegged wooden one, was fixed to a revolving stand and dressed as a pedlar, complete with baskets or tray of tiny wares. She also had a stick with which to point at a number painted on the stand when the base, having been spun round, finally stopped moving. To find out what the future held in store, one merely looked up the fortune written beside the corresponding number in a little book sold with the doll.

Like the Pedlar dolls, the Fortune Tellers could be both commercially and home-made. In an issue of *The Girls' Companion*, published in the late 1840s, full instructions were given for making a fortune-telling doll. A list of fortunes was also thoughtfully provided, all ready to be carefully copied on to the little pastel-coloured folded papers which formed her petticoat.

A German version of a fortune-teller, which appeared in the early 1890s, was made entirely of paper. This 'Orakelpuppe', as it was called, had a multi-pleated skirt with a prediction printed on each fold. Although an intriguing toy, it was more fragile and less ornamental than most of the English variety.

A different kind of surprise was supplied by the Russian Matryushka, or 'nest' doll. This shiny, gaily painted wooden doll pulled apart at the waist to show another, smaller replica, inside. Hidden within that one was another, and so on, down to the last tiny, solid doll. Depending upon the size of the largest doll, five, seven, nine, fifteen, even twenty-one dolls might be lined up in a row before being returned to their nest inside the biggest one again. Although, like the Jack-in-the-box, these could surprise but once, they were always popular toys, perhaps because they are among the few display dolls which are also real playthings; see plate 9.

A similar idea started the making of the Russian man doll ornament: but this opens to reveal a set of wooden ninepins and a ball, not more tiny figures.

Although always thought of as Russian, the nest doll originated in the Far East. It was not until the late 1890s that the popular Russian version, taken from the earlier Chinese design, began to be manufactured in quantity in the toymaking region near Moscow. Ironically, the original Chinese dolls seem to have been forgotten. There is a Japanese kokeshi version, but it is not often seen. In my collection of over one hundred and fifty kokeshi at present there is only one. It is painted to look like a Japanese boy wearing a kimono and contains four diminishing replicas; see page 179.

The English preference, at least in Victorian days, seems to have been for the nest to be a little painted wooden egg which opened to display a minute jointed wooden doll, often less than 2.5 cm (1 in) in height. The egg was often inscribed 'The smallest doll in the world'.

The doll-in-the-egg idea was also popular in central Europe; although there the little dolls were generally tiny, turned, one-piece 'babies', painted to look as if they had been swaddled. Curiously enough this European liking is a complete reversal of the original Chinese idea. There, the innermost item in the nest doll was usually a tiny egg; see page 179.

2

Dolls for Play:
Home-made and folk

The actual material used in making dolls is of little help in their classification, for the same material has been used in so many different ways.

Wood, for instance, has been used for the most expensive and elaborate bespoke dolls, and for the cheapest little item in the street-vendor's tray. The family tree of the Wooden Doll has, so to speak, roots in many lands, On one lowly, but ancient, branch are the totem-like Japanese kokeshi; on another, even lower, the European pegged wooden dolls.

Although all kokeshi are basically shaped like ninepins with loose heads, the permutations of size, style and decoration are seemingly endless – due entirely to the individual craftsman's own design being respected by his fellows. Like all Orientals their expression of the kokeshi is always enigmatic as, indeed, is their position in the doll world, and, to some extent, their history.

It seems that the first kokeshi were made as a side-line by the wood turners of the northeast of Japan early in the Edo period (1614–1868). They were then children's playthings, though originally they may have had a certain religious, or phallic, significance. They are still made by the thousand, sold as souvenirs all over Japan and widely exported. Although popular with children they are nowadays more often collected by adults and used as decorative ornaments, so forming yet another example of the almost impossible task of distinguishing dolls for display from those for play.

Wherever forests grew, there flourished the wood-carvers and turners. Just as the Japanese wood turners made kokeshi at first almost as a hobby so, most probably, did their counterparts in Europe start dollmaking. The carvers of religious statues and figures in the seventeenth century in the Grödner Tal and Bavaria also became famous for their little jointed wooden dolls; the turners in Bohemia used their lathes to make the gaily painted swaddled wooden 'babies', very like the kokeshi in shape; while the Russian carvers of the province of Moscow cut their curiously shaped figures from blocks of wood – again in a style reminiscent of earlier Japanese dollmakers. Perhaps the trade routes to the far East across the Bohemian plains and Russian steppes provide a possible clue to these similarities?

In this cottage industry many carvers and their families were necessary to fulfil the demand for the cheap little wooden dolls with their shiny black painted hair and their pegged joints. In the Tyrol they were made of the local pine and in Bavaria most commonly from lime (linden).

As architects varied the usage of materials for houses, with 'Queen Anne' fronts and 'Mary Anne' backs – that is with expensive, imposing facades and cheaper, functional backs – so, for the same economic reasons, did dollmakers use wood to create two entirely different styles of doll. But while it is relatively easy to compile the genealogy of the grand 'Queen Anne' wooden dolls, that of the thousands of common 'Mary-Annes' is difficult to disentangle. The finer of the early nineteenth-century dolls, with their yellow painted combs and grey-black curls, little pointed faces, sloping shoulders, tiny waists and well-shaped bustlines, are carefully painted and varnished and their limbs well-pegged and articulated. Owing to the strict rules of the all-powerful eighteenth and early nineteenth century guilds, Tyrolean turners might make little dolls, but only the painters, in centres like Berchtesgaden and Oberammergau, could paint them. Later, both making and painting – the latter usually by the women of the villages – were carried out in the mountain regions of the Grödner Tal, and local dealers collected and packed the dolls for export. By the end of the century the little dolls were crudely made, pegged with mere splinters of wood, and daubed rather than painted with the traditional, stylised black hair, red cheeks and red shoes; see plate 11.

Since the late eighteenth century, pedlars had carried wooden toys and dolls from the valleys of the Grödner Tal into Italy and Spain – and even as far as Mexico and the USA, where they sometimes settled. It is interesting to note that the grandfather of the famous Albert Schoenhut, maker of all-wood jointed dolls in America in the 1870s, was carving wooden dolls in Germany in the 1790s. But, by the end of the nineteenth century Grödner dealers, like Herr Purger, were crating millions of little wooden dolls for export. It is recorded that the dealers supplied the women with the dolls to paint and, in the 1870s, paid them a farthing a dozen 'out of which they had to buy the size and paint': the rate for the makers of the dolls was then five farthings (about $\frac{1}{2}$p) a dozen.

Sometimes these dolls are collectively known as 'Peg-dolls', 'pegged-woodens', 'Wooden Bettys' or 'Nürnberg filles', but they are undoubtedly best known as 'Dutch dolls'. As they are all, whatever their age and quality, made of wood and their joints – with one exception – are held in place with little wooden pegs, these are descriptive names. (The exception is the 'Wooden Kate' variety of doll, whose joints consist of tiny strips of leather nailed to the wooden torso and limbs.) As Nürnberg was a well-known centre for dolls, with a famous annual toy fair, that name is not inappropriate. But how has the name of the flattest country in Europe become associated with wooden dolls made in the mountainous regions of Italy, Austria, Bavaria and Germany?

Although it has been suggested often enough that the dolls were called 'Dutch' in error – the word being a corruption of 'Deutsch' (German) which is certainly nearer their place of origin – there is another, and perhaps more logical, explanation. After the local Grödner dealers had crated the dolls they were sent down to the big exporters, the Dutch merchants in such ports as Amsterdam. It was from Holland that they came to England, and as imported Dutch dolls that they were known.

In 'A Tribe of Toymakers', an article which appeared in an 1875 issue of *Leisure Hour*, Margaret Howitt writes: '. . . nearly all these myriads of dolls (from St Ulrich in the Grödner Tal) are for Britain. Those larger dolls' heads, it is true, are destined for Amsterdam, but they merely rest there *to receive bodies and the title of Dutch dolls*, after which they resume their journey to become aunts and mothers to the lesser dolls *which have already crossed the British Channel*' (the italics are mine).

The reference to receiving bodies may seem a little puzzling as it certainly does not conjure up the picture of the traditional Dutch doll epitomised in Florence Upton's pictures in *The Adventures of Two Dutch Dolls and a Golliwog* (1895). But it must be remembered that many wooden doll busts were also made in the Grödner Tal, with the characteristic Dutch doll looks as well as with more natural looking faces; and, in those days, any doll with a wooden head imported from Holland would be known as a Dutch doll; see page 175.

Leisure Hour certainly seems to confirm that the only connections these 'Dutch dolls' had with Holland were of the marketing and not the manufacturing kind; and that, in the case of the smaller dolls, the sole connection was in transit.

It must not be forgotten, however, that a fair number of these little dolls were not only hawked round the streets of London, but were also made there.

By the middle of the nineteenth century England had a flourishing indigenous populace of 'Mary-Annes' as well as the surviving grand antique 'Queen Anne' dolls. Common little dolls the former may have been, coming from such addresses as Twister's Alley or Bunhill Row, but they and their continental cousins found their way into palaces as well as cottages, and provided much joy to the young Princess Victoria as well as to her future subjects.

America – North and South – has an enormous heritage of folk dolls. In the North, this is probably due to the number of poor immigrants who brought memories and inherited skills with them to the New World, even if few managed to include the children's actual dolls in their luggage. It is fascinating – if at times confusing – to try and trace these links with the old world among the array of American regional dolls.

One of the best known of North American dolls is the 'shuck' or corn-husk doll. It is usually stated that, in return for the English wooden dolls distributed as gifts by the colonists in 1585, the North American Indians taught the settlers how to make their own traditional corn-husk dolls. But was this always the case? Shuck dolls probably were made – the tribes certainly used other natural materials, such as clay, wood, leather and feathers, when they made dolls – but compare the two husk dolls in plate 13 with the husk doll in plate 12. The former are traditional ones made in Czechoslovakia.

Again, it is true that the Seminole Indians used fibre – in their case from coconuts – in dollmaking, but so did the Russians. If the little Russian doll in plate 13, which is made from flax fibre, is compared with the Seminole doll and the Tennessee husk-and-fibre dolls, the true family history is questionable to say the least.

Another 'typically American' doll, the painted pinewood doll attributed to Pennsylvania, bears an uncanny likeness to the 'Bartholomew babies' once sold at London's most notorious fair.

It is interesting to speculate about the influence of heredity and environment on these dollmakers: the schoolmarm, Hickory Nuthead, has relatives all over the world; the apple-head doll from the mid-west – surely his family tree has roots in Europe? And let us also remember the corn-cob 'Indian doll' – so very like the corn-cob dolls made by the Zulu and Kaffirs in Africa; see plate 12.

These cross-cultural influences continue in the modern counterparts of the old-timers. In 1958 'Lilli', a newspaper cartoon character, inspired a Bavarian doll firm to make a Lilli doll; in 1959 Mattel, the big American toy manufacturing company, bought the prototype and launched their version as 'Barbie', so that this famous doll is, in effect, an identical 'daughter' of Lilli.

Between the demise of the German Lilli and her rebirth as the American Barbie she made a brief but curious appearance in England. I first saw the dolls decorating a chain of shoe-shop's windows in the West Country. On returning to London, I found a small cache of them in, of all places, Woolworths and, being interested in dolls used for advertising, bought one. It will be amusing to see if Lilli ever has a 'grand-daughter', and in which country she will appear – she has 'sisters' in Hong Kong already.

The magnificent fur-clad Eskimo in plate 13 could only have come from one region. Entirely made of leather and fur, he represents the son of an important member of the community – a chief in any other tribe – wearing a winter costume. The 'harness' of lichen-dyed leather, the triangular pattern of the fur edging the tunic, are symbols of his status. His boots are worn with the fur inside for extra warmth, and because the roughened suede soles help prevent slipping on the ice. The long-haired fur hood is a vital winter garment as the hairs help to 'warm', or at least filter, the icy air before the wearer breathes it in.

South America, of course, has a range of very different dollmaking materials, although a few of the primitive tribes use animal bones for dolls, much as the Eskimos use walrus tusks. Clay and cloth dolls were more usually made, particularly in Peru – which also has some of the rare South American wooden dolls. Far more common, towards the north, are dolls of plaited palm leaves, straw, and hard, painted leather. Most of these dolls represent ordinary country folk and street vendors are particular favourites; see plate 12.

Paper, though of course fragile, has always been a popular medium for those making dolls in the cheaper range. Flocked papers, crêpé, tissue, metallic, plain, textured and patterned papers provide endless permutations for the makers of paper dolls, and have been used for many years by both Eastern and Western designers.

The Japanese, who regard paper as suitable for building purposes, fanmaking and many other artistic creations, naturally used it for dollmaking. *Anesama-ningyō* have flat bodies, made of coloured, patterned papers, but their heads, with elaborate paper hairstyles, are three-dimensional. Usually the heads are little paper balls but, in the famous dollmaking district of Matsue, clay moulded round a little bamboo-stick is preferred. These dolls apparently originated about the middle of the Edo period (1614–1868), during the heyday of very elaborate styles of hairdressing in Japan. This probably explains why, though the body is simple and the face often completely blank, the dolls' hairstyles are extremely complicated and ornamental. The example in plate 14 has been posed to show this blank face; but the correct Japanese way to display these dolls is to show their back view, as in this way the head-dresses are seen to their best advantage.

However, these dolls were made originally as playthings, and not for display. They were used as a kind of doll's house doll in the game of *mamagoto asobi* (playing house), in which the dolls enacted the roles of hostess, maid servants and guests. In this they also served an educational purpose somewhat similar to the hina-ningyō.

Although the medium is the same, the technique and design of the two Western examples of paper dolls in the same photograph, plate 14, are completely different. The Scottish designer of the Highlander has created a lifelike figure. A wire framework has been made and covered with crêpé paper and the face and the authentic tartan have been meticulously painted with watercolours to achieve a most realistic effect.

On the other hand the maker of the little Polish doll has chosen to produce a more stylised doll, although the work that has gone into its making is equally skilled. Not only is every little flower bordering her skirt hand cut, but every one of the narrow stripes is a separate strip of thin, coloured paper pasted on to a plain, stiffer base. The paper used for the doll's head and body is similar to the white paper once used for lining drawers and cupboards, while the paper for the sleeves and head kerchief is a little thicker than tissue. The Poles are traditionally famous for cut-paper work, and this little doll clearly demonstrates how effectively the dollmaker has adapted the idea for his craft.

In 1746 France was swept by an absolute mania for 'Pantins', little flat pasteboard figures whose movable limbs jerked frantically when a string was pulled. Not all were Jumping Jacks, since some charming peasant girls and ballerinas delighted both adults and children alike. Eventually the little dolls were forbidden by law – the excuse being that women, through playing with them, might conceive children with jerking limbs *à la* Pantin!

To England must go the credit of producing a popular, and more lasting, paper plaything. Although printed sheets of figures to cut out had been sold in Europe for some time, it was an English designer who produced the first true paper doll, complete with sets of clothes, for children – a completely different idea from the continental cut-out fashion sheets designed for adults. In 1780 Parson Woodforde recorded in his diary the gift he had made to a little girl of a paper doll 'with several dresses to it', proof that they had become a general plaything by that time.

By the 1840s these toys were being exported to the USA and also designed and commercially made there. During the late 1850s and 1860s dolls of famous people were particularly popular, and by the late 1890s there were paper dolls of all descriptions, flat, folded, with cone shaped or 'honeycomb' skirts, in seemingly endless variety.

But although several French and German firms designed paper dolls in imitation of 'the English doll', as a German journal referred to them in 1791, most of the famous paper dolls for children were created by English firms, among whom Raphael Tuck's name is perhaps the best known. From the 1890s until World War II their novelty paper dolls and books were popular at home and abroad.

One particularly ingenious example of Tuck's dolls is number 135 in the firm's Royal 'Art Novelty' Series. Under the heading 'In Dolly Land' the box-lid label states that inside is 'a marvellous arrangement of 48 dressed dolls, all interchangeable, producing no less than 2304 distinct changes . . . to change the dress of any doll, draw the head gently sideways through the slit in the costume, and re-insert in the same way into any other costume'.

A box of these dolls recently came into my possession, with the original seller's label, 'Sold by W. Whiteley, Stationer etc., Westbourne Grove' and the price, 'Nine pence half-penny [4p]', still clearly visible on the underneath of the box well over half a century later. The little dolls, as may be seen by looking carefully at the one lying flat in plate 15, have four printed costumes, two on each double side of the thin pasteboard, and a snake-like strip, with two pairs of printed faces each end of it, is inserted through the communal neck opening. One such four-in-one doll can be seen as 'The Prim Doll' and 'Dolly at the Fancy Dress Ball' on one double side, and be reversed to produce 'A Black Dolly' and 'Red Riding-Hood'.

In the same photograph are two examples of another English speciality, a little book containing 'A Moral Tale for Little Children', a set of cut-out costumes and one removable head with which to make a popular doll of the hero or heroine of the story.

The History and Adventures of Little Henry, exemplified in a series of figures, written by Doctor Walcot was first published in 1810, by S. and J. Fuller. In the same year they also published *The History of Little Fanny* and several other similar works. Both Little Fanny and Little Henry seem to have been far more popular than poor little *Ellen, or the Naughty Girl Reclaimed* – a not altogether surprising discovery bearing in mind the tender age of the readers.

Somewhat akin to paper dolls, in that so many were printed on flat surfaces ready to be cut out, were the more substantial dolls generally known as 'Rag'. Rag dolls – those made from all kinds of fabrics and stuffed with some soft filling – have a long history. They have been found in children's tombs from the ancient civilisations of Egypt, Rome and Peru, while children in India, China, and South and North America all played with rag dolls of one kind or another long before traders or colonists arrived with their European examples.

Although all the early ones were home made, commercial rag dolls became very popular during the nineteenth century. These might either be already stuffed, or sold with the doll pieces printed on fabric ready for the buyer to cut out and sew. This form is still as popular today as it was in the 1890s, when firms like Dean's Rag Company in England and the Arnold Print Works in the USA manufactured such dolls by the thousand.

Some of the most famous late nineteenth-century designers of stiffened rag dolls, or dolls reinforced in some way with cloth, were American, such as Izannah Walker, Ludwig Greiner and Martha Chase.

The USA also produced one of the best-loved of all rag dolls. In 1915 a patent was issued to Johnny Gruelle for a doll labelled 'Raggedy Ann'; see plate 16. According to the book of *Raggedy Ann Stories* that he wrote, the original heroine had belonged to his mother when she was a child. With a little help the doll certainly took to her famous heart the old commandment to be fruitful and multiply as, today, Raggedy Ann dolls, books, ornaments, printed materials and so on flourish on both sides of the Atlantic.

During the nineteenth century southern Russia was well known for its hand-made fabric dolls with beautifully embroidered faces and regional costumes. They were usually sold in pairs, a man and a woman. The little nineteenth-century doll held by Raggedy Ann, plate 16, is actually from Bulgaria, but the design is very similar, and she is unusual only because she has red hair – a colour not usually given to dolls.

The two little dolls in Russian dress are from a set showing all the regional costumes of the USSR. They are made, not from compressed paper, but rags, which hold dye very much better and thus give the dolls a brighter look.

The three little characters in plate 14 display an interesting blend of fabric and paper in their construction. Japanese dollmakers have always been faced with the problem that, if they dress their dolls accurately in all the layers of an authentic Japanese costume, the finished effect is very cumbersome, and not at all like the delicate, graceful creations they had in mind.

Furthermore, the smaller the doll, the more difficult was the problem. However, the designers of such dolls solved it in two ways. First, the dolls' bodies and limbs were reduced to little more than a framework. This was then dressed in the outer garments and the under garments were suggested by attaching to the outer ones only those parts which actually showed. The little 'stick' doll, plate 14, displaying the silk and brocade costume has had her slimming treatment carried out to the point of emaciation. Her body is, as her name suggests, just a stick, her head only a little ball of padded silk; but the finished doll effectively presents a charming, immaculately-attired appearance.

The art of sticking fabrics to padded paper figures is known to have been recorded in Japan at least as early as the beginning of the eighteenth century. Unfortunately the provenance of the two European versions in the same photograph is not so easy to discover. The printed pasteboard figures, mounted on wooden blocks, have slightly padded bodies, and their costumes have been exquisitely made from thin silk, the narrowest of ribbons and minute beads. Possibly they were made by some talented amateur 'somewhere in central Europe' during the nineteenth century. The clothes, at all events, look very 'middle-European', and the little figures themselves could very easily have been cut-outs from some book or magazine, or else commercially designed ones. Judging by the tiny beads and the width of the ribbons, as well as the style of the figures themselves, they are probably mid-Victorian.

Truly has it been said that a doll can be made from practically anything and Käthe Kruse, so legend has it, made her first doll from a potato and a towel filled with sand. Her husband, a well-known sculptor in Berlin, detested the stiff, formal dolls their children played with, and so Käthe Kruse began experimenting to find a way to make a doll which would not only look, but handle like a baby.

In 1910, after four year's work, she allowed her dolls to be shown in public; their childlike appeal and posture, not to mention their durability and washable quality, attracted immediate orders. All the dolls she designed, the babies and little girls and boys, were all made with a specially prepared muslin head, stiffened and painted to give a most natural look to the doll, and a chubby body, very firmly made. Frau Professor Kruse supervised the making of all her dolls: each stage of production had to have her approval, and the finished results bear witness to her care.

Production of these dolls began just before World War I, and just before World War II the first Käthe Kruse mannequin dolls appeared in shop windows. In 1955 her designs were reproduced by a German plastics firm – this is the version shown in plate 17. Although Käthe Kruse died in 1968 her business goes on; it is now, under the management of her children, in Donauwörth whither she had moved it shortly after the end of World War II.

Today Käthe Kruse's dolls bear little resemblance to the potato in which they had their origin. Equally interesting stories lie behind 'General Gordon' and 'La Parisienne' – plates 18 and 19 – whose names do seem, at first glance, a little unlikely.

Some seventy years ago Andrew Morrison, a Scottish chief engineer, was working with the Bengal and North Western Railway. After his son's birth he asked a local craftsman to make a toy horse and a rider for the boy, suggesting 'Chinese' Gordon, plate 18, as he was often called, as a likely subject. It is hardly surprising that the man thought the traditional yellowish varnish, so often used on Indian folk-toys, particularly appropriate for this soldier – even if he wondered, privately, at the decidedly un-Chinese uniform the Scotsman requested him to make! India has a strong dollmaking tradition, but this horse's construction is unusually interesting. Soft muslin has been stretched and pasted over the carved animal – except over the saddle and bridle – before it was painted, but the General seems to have been painted and varnished without the use of any fabric – apart from the silk tassel on his fez which, for some inexplicable reason, seems to have been more durable than his right arm and leg.

The Arab dolls round the Egyptian guide on plate 19 are good examples of contemporary dolls in traditional costumes. The guide himself is more unusual, being a fabric doll of great character. But, as he is no doubt explaining, it is La Parisienne herself who is most worthy of attention. I am indebted to an Egyptian friend, Josephine Conrad-Wissa, not only for the doll, but for this account of its creation:

In the remote village of Esneh, south of Asswan, is to be found an aged dollmaker – the last craftsman, perhaps, to practise this art in the whole of Egypt. He is very old, rheumy, and completely illiterate – living in a simple mud hut, surrounded by wives, children, chickens, rabbits and pigeons – happily making his 'folk-art' dolls. The body shape is very primitive, rather star-fish like and reminiscent of the earliest Egyptian wooden dolls, having the same long neck and very short arms. The doll's features are crudely embroidered, and the costume seems to be a cross between Berber (elaborate neck and nose ornaments) and Bedouin (face veil and dress heavily sequinned). The doll has great allure, and the added charm of being completely unlike the commercially mass-produced dolls found in all Egyptian souvenir shops.

The most curious thing, though, is that the old man, who has never been further, in all probability, than the outskirts of the village, calls his creation 'La Parisienne'! Obviously, the fact that this city constituted the Mecca of Fashion, and the epitome of all that is chic and elegant, has reached out even as far as Esnah; therefore, in the proud dollmaker's opinion, his cherished creation could bear no fitter name!

3 Dolls for Play: Commercial western dolls

If the last group of play dolls seemed to get 'curiouser and curiouser' these dolls remain firmly this side of the nursery looking-glass. With the discovery of new materials, and the increasing use of machinery from the mid-nineteenth century onwards, the number of commercially mass-produced dolls greatly increased in Europe and the USA.

Pre-plastic – using the word in its contemporary sense – commercial dolls could be made of many substances, and still be described by the manufacturers as 'unbreakable'.

Wood, of course, is the most obvious material, and has been used by dollmakers throughout the world for centuries. In the Western world there are three distinct varieties of wooden doll: the cheap turned and carved European 'folk' dolls; the more expensive, earlier English 'Queen Anne' type doll and, from 1911, the American 'Schoenhut all wood perfection art doll'.

This last, the 'Doll wonder of the twentieth century . . . universally acknowledged to be the greatest invention in the history of dolls' – according to the manufacturer's catalogue – was 'the strongest and most indestructible . . . fully jointed . . . artistic manikin doll . . . superior to any jointed figure ever produced.' The makers went on to describe, with equal modesty, the three types made, 'Character', 'Doll-face' and 'Window Display', as 'the best dolls in the world today'. Be that as it may, Schoenhut dolls were certainly popular, combining as they did, natural-looking faces with fully-articulated mbs. These were jointed with steel spring-hinges and could hold ny number of natural poses; see page 179.

There were other Schoenhut dolls: in 1903 Albert Schoenhut had roduced the Humpty Dumpty Circus dolls and toys, and, after his eath in 1912, the factory went on making dolls under the direction f his sons until the 1920s.

Other wood-and-metal dolls had been designed in the USA as ar back as the 1870s by Joel Ellis, the founder of the Springfield toy ompany in Vermont.

Rubber never achieved the popularity of the other 'unbreakable' naterials used for dollmaking. However, some dolls were made of oft rubber as early as the 1840s, and when in 1851 Charles Goodyear ook out his patent for vulcanised rubber in the USA, several lesigners, such as Mademoiselle Rohmer, experimented with it luring the 1850s. Even European doll companies of the stature of chilling and Bru created at least one line of rubber dolls during the 870s, when several attempts were made to improve the durability nd colouring of the material. But children never seemed to find ubber dolls as attractive as their other playthings – possibly the mell had something to do with this lack of enthusiasm.

Rubber dolls did have a revival in the 1930s when so many baby lolls were made to be bathed, and even 'fed'. The American 'Dy-dee 3aby', produced by Fleischaker and Baum (Effanbee), wet its nappy hortly after taking a drink from its feeding bottle. Rubber was the bvious choice for this type of doll, and the quality had much mproved by this date.

Herr Lippert, the designer of so many American dolls, disliked the ace of this particular creation so much that he implored Hugo 3aum not to use it, saying it was 'the dumbest face he ever worked ip'. Happily, from the point of view of countless little American irls, Baum took no notice, and the 'Dy-dee Baby' swept straight nto second place in the 1936 sales chart, being beaten only by the ver popular 'Shirley Temple' doll.

In 1855 celluloid had been invented by an Englishman, Alexander Parkes, after whom it was called Parkesine. But it was the American Hyatt brothers, founders of the Celluloid Novelty Company in 1869, who subsequently started manufacturing celluloid dolls sometime during the 1870s. The USA seems to have produced most of the celluloid dolls from the 1870s until about 1900. From then on although French firms also used it, German manufacturers took the lead. Kestner, Kämmer and Reinhardt, C. and O. Dressel all made celluloid dolls, but perhaps the best-known firm was the Rheinische Gumm und Celluloid Fabrik Company, whose turtle-in-a-diamond trade mark was stamped on so many doll necks and bodies from 1889 onwards.

Between the wars Poland and Japan also produced celluloid dolls. The little Japanese versions of kewpies, see p. 37, and other small dolls were particularly popular and were exported to Europe and the USA by the million.

Many celluloid and metal doll heads were exported from Germany to distributors in England and the USA, who then attached them to stuffed or composition bodies. Thus it is perfectly possible to have an 'original' doll with a celluloid or metal head, kid body, bisque hands and composition legs and feet.

Painted brass or pewter was sometimes used for doll heads, but tin, with some form of coating, was more usual. Three of the best known lines of tin doll heads were made by Vischer and Heller in Germany, who made 'Minerva' and 'Diana' heads shortly before the turn of the century, and by Standfuss whose 'Juno' appeared shortly after. At about this time the Metal Doll Company of the USA began to make all-metal, jointed, dolls in addition to their range of metal doll heads; see plate 20.

Still 'unbreakable' but softer all over were the velvet and felt dolls of the Chad Valley and Norah Welling firms in England, and the Lenci factory in Italy.

Chad Valley, which from the early twenties was the name of the old firm of Johnson Brothers Ltd founded in 1860, manufactured dolls made of partially stiffened felt. Some of their most successful lines were the doll versions of the cheeky, cherubic children drawn by the illustrator Mabel Lucie Attwell.

Although this firm was influenced by contemporary artists it is not certain whether the Scavinis firm reacted in the same way with their dolls. Enrico Scavini and his wife, Elena, used her pet-name of 'Lenci' as the trade-mark for their dolls. These were made of pressed felt, the faces having painted features.

The doll dressed as 'Christopher Robin' in plate 21 does look remarkably like A. A. Milne's famous character, but, as this particular doll's smock is his only genuine 1920s garment, it is difficult to be sure. Browsing through an Oxfam shop a few years ago I saw a pair of doll's legs sticking out of a tub of oddments and automatically pulled the doll out to rescue it. My delight at finding a Lenci doll in such an unlikely place was intensified on discovering the price – 35p!

The endearing 'Piglet' was the result of seeing a newspaper article about the maker of the original 'Winnie-the-Pooh' characters for A. A. Milne's son. An exchange of letters followed – and the most welcome Piglet. Although unseen in the photograph, Pooh addicts will be glad to know that 'Small' is also there, climbing up Piglet's back.

These 'soft' dolls made ideal play dolls, being capable of accepting fairly rough treatment without damage to themselves, and without any sharp or breakable parts to injure the child.

The next group of dolls is a contrast to those appearing in plate 21. 'All-bisques' is the descriptive collective term for those dolls made with head, body and limbs of unglazed ware. Because 'bisque' and 'china' have many meanings in different contexts perhaps it should be noted that, in dollmaking, bisque means unglazed tinted ware, and china the fixed ware once it has been glazed; see plate 22.

Without going into unnecessary detail it should also be mentioned that the terms bisque and china must be sub-divided at least once or twice to achieve even a rough description of the dolls of that particular type.

The lowest quality bisque, containing some of the clay's original impurities such as feldspar, is somewhat loosely described as 'stoneware'. This type of ware was used for cheap little dolls' house dolls around the turn of the century. Bisque usually describes dolls with their heads, at least, made of unglazed but decorated (that is tinted and painted) ware.

'Parian' is really a complete misnomer. Parian ware was a pure white, finely textured bisque, invented by the English firm of Copeland's in the early 1850s and looking like the dense white marble from the island of Paros. Parian dolls, therefore, would have to be completely free of any colouring if this description was to be helpfully accurate. However, the term is loosely used to describe dolls with painted features, but a very dense white 'complexion'.

China dolls are dolls made wholly or partially from glazed, fired ware. The finest quality china containing kaolin, the super-fine white clay, is referred to as 'porcelain'. This is the description given to dolls whose heads, if not also their limbs, were made at such fine porcelain works as Meissen. Porcelain doll heads are thinner, and therefore lighter in weight, than china, and the quality of the doll is also apparent in the finely cut features.

Three of the dolls photographed are bisque; the one standing 'like Patience on a monument' has a china front and a stone-ware back and is surely one of the doll designers' dottier ideas. Made with an unglazed back to enable the doll to float in water, this fragile 'Bath-doll' would have broken into several alarmingly sharp pieces at the slightest knock against anything other than a rubber bath-tub. If really used as a water toy, as its name suggests, it must surely rank as one of the most dangerous playthings ever created. There are some more sturdy, completely glazed versions, but they seem to have been designed to stand in a doll's bath, rather than to float in a child's at bath-time. In the USA these dolls are also known as 'Frozen Charlottes' – apparently after the legendary vain young girl who froze to death in an open sleigh because she would not cover her beautiful dress with a warm cloak. The English, less poetically inclined perhaps, and seeing not a stitch of clothing let alone a ball-dress on the doll, stick firmly to the no-nonsense 'bath-doll' for the larger versions. The little inch-long ones remain, for us, 'Pudding dolls' for, in the 'Good Old Days' no Christmas pudding worthy of its brandy would have been without its bright silver sixpence or threepenny bit, it thimble, 'gold' ring and tiny china doll to excite, and very possibly choke, the children on Christmas Day.

The two dressed children are fully articulated at the shoulders and hips, being strung with elastic cord. The head and torso of the all-bisque baby is moulded in one piece and the toddler has a bisque head, which fits into the socket neck of his heavier ceramic body. The baby doll is unmarked, and the only letters on the toddler doll, DEP, merely stand for *déposé* in French and *deponirt* in German meaning 'registered'. Most probably both were made by the German doll company of Gebrüder Heubach, as DEP in a diamond is generally accepted as a Heubach mark.

Sometimes such all-bisques were made as 'one-piece dolls' without joints, more often they had jointed arms, if not always arm and leg joints, while some were fully articulated.

The fine quality of these small dolls is evident. They were also extremely varied, ranging from natural-looking children, made mainly in Germany and France, to characters like the 'Kewpies', which originated in the USA.

Rose O'Neill created the Kewpies originally as impish little creatures for magazine illustrations. In 1912 she applied for a patent, and the distributing company of George Borgfeldt, who held the production and distribution rights, registered the trade-mark 'Kewpie' in England and France in 1913. The actual dolls were designed by Joseph Kallus, an artist employed by Borgfeldt to work with Rose O'Neill on the production of the first Kewpie dolls. Later, in 1916, Kallus founded his own Rex Doll Company, and his firm was one of several who made Kewpies under licence for Borgfeldt. Other manufacturers in the USA included the Fulper Pottery, who made them in bisque, and the Mutual Doll Company who used composition for theirs. In Europe, where Rose O'Neill went in 1913 to supervise the making of Kewpies by the German firm of Kestner, the Kewpie craze was equally strong. Standfuss, who made the celluloid Kewpies, was but one of the other twenty-odd firms in Germany alone who, by 1914, were producing standing, sitting, lying, clothed and unclothed Kewpies in all materials.

Japan made a series of 'pirate' Kewpies, replicas of some of the best-selling lines. Altogether Kewpies appeared in hundreds of characters and dozens of forms and were one of the most popular dolls ever to achieve world-wide fame.

Another American woman, Martha Chase, also created a best-

37

selling line of commercially produced dolls. She, however, was not professional artist like Rose O'Neill and, in fact, had more in commo with the German Frau Kruse and an earlier resident of her own Rhoc Island, Izannah Walker, who made stiffened rag dolls. All thre women first made dolls for their own children, and it was these whic later served as prototypes for their commercially produced successor

Martha Chase, the wife of a country doctor, made her first dol in the 1880s. She allowed them to be exhibited at a Boston store, an the resultant demand for 'Chase dolls' was so great that, in 1896, th Chase Stockinet Doll Company was formed to cope with the order The dolls made by the company were heavy, with firmly stuffe bodies and stiffened, hand-painted heads. They came in man characters, from Mr Pickwick to George Washington, but it is th Chase children and babies which are the best known; see plate 23.

Some of the Chase dolls are more than playthings. In 1910 th Hartford Hospital ordered a Chase baby doll for use in trainin nurses. Since that time hospitals all over the world have use specially designed 'Chase Hospital dolls' – babies, children an adults – fitted with an internal system of intake and drainage pipes.

Although Chase dolls are of undoubted use and interest, a advertisement for them asking 'Are you looking for a doll that ha beauty and a serious purpose in life', and which goes on to sta solemnly that 'they take their place beside the works of Christophe Wren, Sheraton, Stradivarius and Cellini . . .' might seem to b rather overstating the case.

Another line of home-made dolls, although somewhat less we known, began in the 1880s. Alice le Hurays and Judy Guilles had dollmaking business in Cobo, Guernsey, and named all their pro ducts either 'Cobo-Alice' or 'Cobo-Judy'. Both dolls were made o strong calico with the features crudely outlined in ordinary househol paints: pink for the limbs and head, black or brown for the hair an eyes and red for the lips. If any irate child ever hit another with Cobo doll, it must have seemed to the stunned victim more like lethal weapon than a doll, for they were tightly stuffed with hardwoo sawdust and extremely heavy; see plate 23.

Wax, although it can look exquisitely fragile, is tougher than i ppears to be. In Mediterranean countries, especially Italy, wax has een used for image-making – and possibly, in some areas, for doll-naking – since Biblical times. In countries as far apart as Bavaria, pain, England and Mexico, wax dolls were made in increasing umbers from 1700 onwards. But most of the early varieties were nade as crib figures or had some religious connections, like the wax Christ-Child dolls and effigies of saints used in churches and festival rocessions in all Catholic countries.

The life-size funeral effigies of famous people, and those created by culptors such as Madame Tussaud, could never be mistaken for dolls, ut one type of life-like wax creation could, and probably did, cause certain amount of confusion. During the seventeenth century it was ustomary for a rich mother whose baby had died to have a wax eplica of the dead infant made. Dressed in the baby's robes it would ie, at least for the period of mourning, in a cradle in the mother's oom.

These were certainly not 'baby dolls'. As playthings baby dolls were not generally made before the nineteenth century, and then the early ones were usually straight-legged 'child' dolls dressed as babies n long robes. Not until the mid-nineteenth century, when the Pierotti and Montanari families in England made their famous poured wax dolls, did the baby doll, designed as an infant, become common. The earlier, exquisitely moulded wax babies with well-proportioned, carved infant limbs were made to be displayed in churches in southern European countries, and not for children's nurseries.

It is confusing to read records of eighteenth-century purchases of a wax baby' – which, incidentally, could cry and move its eyes – and another 'wax baby, 3 ft (1 m) high, with diamond earrings' until one remembers that all dolls were called 'babies' until the nineteenth century. It follows from this that all dolls' houses were known as 'baby houses' until that date.

It is as well to remember this earlier definition when reading eighteenth-century reports of trials following criminal offences. Sensational words were apparently spoken by William Higgs in 1733 at the trial of Jane Tinsley, accused of stealing 'fourteen naked babies and one jointed one' – an alarming statement when taken ou of context. 'I found fourteen naked babies in Tinsley's room. know my own babies from any other man's. I swear to my ow work for there's never a man in England that makes such babie beside my self.' With relief, one realises the attraction of even th most inanimate doll.

Apart from the small, hollow and extremely fragile wax dolls which were usually made in England *c.* 1800–50, most European wa dolls, particularly those from the Sonneburg region, had head reinforced with papier mâché or plaster cores. Their bodies were o calico or muslin, stuffed with straw, mohair or sawdust, and thei arms, before wax limbs became so popular, were usually of wood o kid coloured fuchsia, ivory, brown or blue. This gave the doll th appearance of wearing gloves, which during the period *c.* 1800–20 had only three fingers. Later ones had the more usual complement o four fingers and a thumb.

Three popular lines sold during the nineteenth century ar illustrated in plate 24. The largest doll in the centre was a favourit type from about 1820–40. She was probably made in Germany, anc is rather larger and better made than the usual 'Bagman's baby' (th dolls sold by the itinerant pedlars and hawkers in England). The othe descriptive, but repellent, name for this doll is 'slit-head', a reference to the slit cut down the head and in which the wig was inserted. Thi frequently resulted in tiny cracks appearing which later caused th 'crazing' effect on so many of these dolls' faces. The shoulder-typ head, common to this kind of doll, is reinforced with plaster, whil her arms are of fuchsia-coloured kid.

The doll in the flowered print dress has a hollow head, ivory 'gloves' – with five fingers – and real hair, inset into the wax scalp with a hot needle and roller. Her most treasured possession is the scrap of paper which gives her provenance. She was bought with three other dolls, one of which was an early wax baby doll lying in a little wicker cradle. Under the pillow was a folded piece of writing-paper which informed me that it was 'EJG's favourite doll, given to her by her Grandmother Elizabeth Glaisque (*née* Horne b. 1775) when she was a very little girl . . . and "Hibernia" [the doll in the

40

print dress] dressed and given to her by her Aunt, then Elizabeth Glaisque, and Aunt Elizabeth's baby doll. The cradle came from her Aunt Sarah Glaisque, who knitted the counterpane and made the sheets. They were sent to her when she was recovering from diptheria and seemed to lose her sight.' Mercifully the note has a rather touching postscript, 'it came back again when she got better'. According to the date marked with the initials EJG, on the sheets, the dolls were given to the small invalid in 1855.

The doll sitting in a striped dress, has a head of wax over papier mâché or composition fitted on to a straw-filled muslin body. Her feet and arms, with hands known as 'spoon-shaped', are painted wood. Her eyes open and shut with a weighted mechanism. (The earlier method of moving a doll's eyes involved pulling a wire, which protruded in a rather indelicate way from the doll's body, to shut the eyes, and pushing it to open them.) She also has a 'squeaker' voice-box. The hair is moulded and painted under the wax covering, and it is this moulding and colouring which gives such dolls their nickname of 'Pumpkin-headed'. This particular doll is probably of German make, as the moulded style was the usual choice for the cheaper range of dolls made from about 1840–60. The black hair-band painted across its head suggests that the doll's head was a late one, made after the publication of Lewis Carroll's *Alice in Wonderland* in 1865, because after that date every little girl wanted an 'Alice band' for her own and her doll's hair. Her shoes, however, are the little flat-heeled bootees which were going out of fashion by that time 'in real life'. But so many dolls' heads were made independently of the bodies that it is quite possible the assembly line had to fix modern heads on to older stock bodies, so that the doll has an ultra-fashionable head and slightly old-fashioned toes.

It was in England, where the wax doll had always been more popular than anywhere else, that the late nineteenth-century doll-makers created the wax dolls that became world-famous. These were the expensive, beautifully dressed, 'poured wax' dolls. In this method the heads and limbs of the dolls are made by pouring liquid wax into moulds, letting it form a skin and then draining off the surplus wax so that the finished product is hollow. Because of the quality of these dolls, which will be discussed in greater detail in the 'Sunday dolls' section, the sale of wax dolls continued in England, though not elsewhere, well into the twentieth century. But, by about 1900, the popularity of the cheaper, less well-made European wax dolls was on the wane.

In the latter part of the nineteenth century dolls in national costumes became very popular. They were of a far better quality than the modern tourist souvenir costume doll, and were made, it seemed, in as many different materials as there were countries.

As the dolls in plates 26 and 27 demonstrate, they were not always made in the country they represented. The Dutch Boy was made in Germany at the factory of Heinrich Zwanzger, Nürnburg, in the 1930s. The body is of pink calico, tightly stuffed, the head is stiffened and has painted hair and features.

The woman supporting the two males wears a provincial French costume and has the mark FG on the shoulders. From the doll's construction it would seem these initials refer to F. Gaultier rather than the other French dollmaking firm of F. (or J.) Gesland, who were also making dolls around 1860–1916. The doll's head is of bisque, with glass eyes and a mohair wig. The body is stuffed and the hands are of a coarser bisque than the head.

The little Scot has a composition head, matt painted features, and inset glass eyes, a stuffed body and shiny composition hands and lower legs. His wig is a mass of tiny curls and is made of lamb's skin. This little doll is typical of its kind, with disproportionately short arms and sewn or pinned-on clothes – only those of the Dutch Boy were made to take off – and it too was probably made in Germany. Dolls dressed as Scots became popular in England following the royal example set by Queen Victoria, whose love of tartan extended to wallpaper and carpets.

The Chinese doll is the kind made for export. Children in 'old' China did not play with dolls which were regarded, as their name even now suggests, more as idols than as playthings. This doll has the traditional long arms and proportionately even longer fingers, and provides a good contrast to the coolie type of doll always dressed in blue or black.

42

The playful Japanese infant is in marked contrast to the stately Chinese although both have in common the fact they were actually made in the countries their costumes suggest. Although the Japanese baby is modern, it is made in the same style as the old *Yamato-ningyō* (Yamato being the ancient name for Japan the words only mean Japanese Doll). Originally yamato-ningyō were kimono-clad little girls, often made as silent envoys to be sent abroad as tokens of friendship. Today, both boy and baby yamato-ningyō are made, and this baby, with his traditional rattle, is typical of the commercially produced variety.

In the Western world even companies of the standing of Bru produced lines of rubber or wooden dolls in addition to their usual bisque-headed ones. But in Japan it would be hard to find a master dollmaker who made anything other than the kind of doll his father before him had made. Just as the country wood-turner had his own particular pattern with which to decorate his kokeshi, so the maker of yamato-ningyō expected his son to make similar yamato-ningyō and not dream of experimenting with paper or wood.

The pensive little jointed papier mâché black boy was the fourth of E. J. Glaisque's dolls, and was probably made in Sonneburg. There is an interesting point, however, about the date of this doll, which has the body construction generally referred to as Motschmann. Charles Motschmann was the dollmaker usually credited with this design, which resulted from seeing the Japanese *mitsuore-ningyō* (literally three-bend doll, so-called because the doll is jointed at the head, waist and knees for full movement). The Motschmann body patent was taken out in 1857, two years after he was supposed to have seen the Japanese dolls at the Paris Exposition and been inspired to create his adapted design. But the note accompanying the Glaisque dolls gives 1855 as the date when the dolls were sent to the child, and the sheets in the cradle of one of the baby dolls are definitely marked with the date. Not for the first time one wishes a doll could speak, if only for long enough to tell its life-story; unfortunately not even the 'squeaker' voice-box, still working after a hundred and twenty years, can help! All three of these coloured dolls, as well as the European ones, are wearing their original clothes; see plate 27.

It is often extremely difficult to ascribe dolls with any degree of accuracy. In that 1733 court case William Higgs, the maker of wooden dolls, experienced no difficulty in recognising his own 'babies'. But the growing popular demand for bisque and composition-headed dolls sometimes makes it impossible to assign them to any one maker. In late nineteenth-century Germany, for instance, owing to the prevalent practice of the sub-division of labour, over eighty people might be involved in the making and dressing of one doll, as mentioned in *Chatterbox*, 1893. As *Harper's Bazaar* pointed out in 1884, a retail shopkeeper might import a doll's body (already made up from one maker's torso and another's limbs) from one source; its head (with or without another maker's eyes) from a second, a wig from a third, and then make up the complete doll himself. Sometimes a doll could be sold under one trade-name, with its head impressed with another mark and its body stamped with a third. If the doll was dressed for the retailer before sale, the number of makers involved increases still further.

Even at source of manufacture there is a complication. Many firms who exported the complete wigged and dressed doll themselves had previously exported or imported parts of it. For example, Simon and Halbig in Germany might send their doll heads to France, to be fitted on to kid bodies and dressed as only the French can dress a doll. Are the dolls then French or German? At the same time Kämmer and Reinhardt were using bisque heads from Simon and Halbig – and celluloid heads from the R.G. and C.F. Company – on 'their' dolls. When one remembers also that many dolls were sold in other countries under the name of the distributor who merely imported them, it is easy to understand why doll historians sometimes wince at the mere mention of the word research.

It can be said, with some confidence, that all four dolls, and the four matching dolls in plates 28 and 29 were made in Germany, probably during the period 1890–1910. Simon and Halbig were among the very first firms to manufacture coloured bisque dolls, calling them in their advertisements 'Dolls of Four Races'. But, although all four of the big dolls in plates 28 and 29 have the letters S. and H. incised on their necks, only three were made by Simon and

Halbig. The fourth, the oriental doll, was made by Shoenau and Hoffmeister, another German firm – which was also known as Porzellan-fabrik Burggrub. Many of its dolls bear the mark of the letters PB contained within a five-pointed star.

Simon and Halbig, in addition to bisque doll heads, also made all-bisque dolls, and composition as well as celluloid dolls' heads. They were one of the best-known German firms, with a prolific output from the 1870s to the late 1920s. One particular design credited to this firm is the best 'flirting eyes' mechanism hitherto produced. The device moved the doll's eyes sideways as well as up and down, opening and closing, on the same weight. Both the European and the Indian dolls have these eyes; their little dolls, however, merely stare straight ahead.

Although the German Armand Marseille dolls are less highly prized by collectors, the firm did make some very good 'character' dolls, notably their 'talking-bisque' girl and the child-doll marked GB. It has not been firmly established whether or not the GB mark was incised on dolls made for the doll-distributing firm of George Borgfeldt. But certainly Armand Marseilles dolls were handled in the USA by Borgfeldt, one of the biggest doll importers from the 1880s until the 1920s. At one time they had exclusive rights in the USA and Canada on Käthe Kruse, Kammer and Reinhardt, Handwerk and Kestner dolls, to name but a few. This firm also, of course, handled American dolls, one of their most famous lines being the Kewpies.

Armand Marseilles dolls were prolifically manufactured from the 1860s to the late 1920s, and they also made doll heads for firms like Louis Amberg and Arranbee. Two of their best-known lines were the 'Floradora' dolls, made for Borgfeldt in 1901, and, of course, the ubiquitous best-seller, 'My Dream Baby', first distributed in 1924. The dolls shown in plate 30 are the original My Dream Baby and the coloured version. Both are idealised infant dolls, and they were made in sizes ranging from a few inches in height to life-size. The 'pretty little darlings' made by Armand Marseille were regarded by adults as being most suitable playthings for their children, but the more realistic portrayals of young babies were not so favoured.

The one exception was the 'Bye-lo Baby'. This doll was created in 1922 by an American, Grace Putnam, who worked from life, using a three-day-old baby model to produce her original wax copy. Owing to certain production problems – largely occasioned by the actual bisque doll heads being made in Germany by such manufacturers as Kling, Kestner and Nertel – Borgfeldt, the distributors, did not achieve a nation-wide promotion for the Bye-lo Baby until about 1925. But, from then on, sales rocketed, earning the doll the title of 'The million dollar baby'; see plate 31.

The original Bye-lo Babies had soft bodies. But little all-bisque ones were also produced later, in 1925, and many copies, authorised and unauthorised, were sold of the Bye-lo Babies which, by then, had been made in everything from wood to celluloid.

If, during the 1920s, My Dream Baby and the Bye-lo Baby were rivals in popularity, the latter was considered far too ugly, or too life-like, by most fond mothers to be played with as a baby doll. Consequently fewer Babies than Dream Babies were made, and they are now valued far more highly by collectors. However, it was quite a popular doll when it was first produced in 1909. Following a minor slump in doll production Kammer and Reinhardt commissioned an artist to produce a 'real baby' model for a new line to be called 'Character Dolls'. The result was a Baby head which was then fixed to a new development, a bent-limb composition baby-doll body. The result was a natural-looking bisque-headed baby doll, one of the first to be marketed, and the response to this innovation was heartening. Later, of course, when the novelty had worn off and other baby dolls were being made with bent limbs, there was a demand for a prettier doll.

But the original Baby had been popular enough to be frequently copied. One of the best-known copies was an unbreakable American adaptation called 'Baby Bumps'. This was made in 1912 for Horsmans 'Can't break 'em' range of composition-headed dolls.

It is, perhaps, a little misleading to talk of bisque or china dolls when referring to those whose only ceramic parts may be their heads. The bodies of these dolls were usually stuffed kid or fabric. Later, towards the turn of the century, jointed wood or composition-

46

bodied dolls were more general. Both the glazed and unglazed heads were produced with painted and often moulded hair, but it is usually the bisque dolls who wear wigs, made of real hair or mohair, as it was thought that hair looked better surrounding a matt, natural-looking face. China or porcelain dolls, however, needed the high gloss of glazed and moulded hair styles.

The two examples of bisque-headed dolls in plate 25 show the fine moulding and colouring of the late nineteenth-century or early twentieth-century baby-dolls. Since fashions tend to change in dolls as in clothes, they are far removed from the 'dolly' looking waxes of previous decades.

The doll in the same plate which appears to be yelling its head off was made by the French firm, SFBJ (*Société Française de Fabrication des Bébés et Jouets*). The Society came into being in 1899, probably because of the successful and ever-increasing export efforts of the German dollmaking firms. The French industry suffered a severe blow in the 1890s, when German dolls were powerful rivals to their erstwhile superiors, and many small French firms were forced out of business. Others consolidated their position by amalgamating, and the group which formed the SFBJ consisted of many famous doll manufacturers, including Jumeau, Bru, Rabery and Delphieu, and Fleischmann and Blödel. The last firm had a branch in Paris, which was sequestred when World War I broke out as Herr Fleischmann, the head of the firm, was judged an alien. That the amalgamation was successful may be judged by the fact that, at the Vincennes factory in 1912, five million dolls were produced before being sent to be dressed in Paris.

The other infant in plate 25 is a German doll, also most probably made about this time, by the firm of Kley and Hahn. It is purely coincidental that the German doll looks as if he realises that he is king of the castle, and that the French doll is protesting so vehemently.

4

Dolls for Play: Sunday best

During Victoria's reign the changes in doll-manufacture and design were probably as great as those in the comparable period after 1901. Remembering this, one soon realises how utterly fatuous the word 'Victorian' really is, when used as a descriptive adjective to cover all the dolls made in this period.

During Victoria's reign the big 'English' wooden dolls became antiques, and there was a marked decline in the quality of the little continental-type jointed wooden dolls. Expensive English poured-wax dolls superseded the cheaper European wax-over-papier mâché variety and bisque-headed dolls rose in popularity as the china-headed ones declined. Rubber dolls took over from gutta-percha; sheets of printed rag-dolls were sold ready to be cut out at home. Celluloid dolls, metal-headed and unbreakable reinforced fabric dolls, parian dolls, all these new dolls were created during Victorian times.

The first lifelike baby dolls were made in this period and 'child' dolls successfully competed against the 'adult' kind, ending their long domination. Dolls' eyes ceased to be moved only by pulling and pushing wires, and began moving on weighted bars fitted within the head. Limbs became more flexible as pegged joints changed to the ball-and-socket type; composition bodies succeeded those of stuffed kid and muslin. Dolls were manufactured which could 'speak' instead of merely squeaking when pressed, and novelty dolls were designed to walk, swim and even 'feed'. There were also lines of dolls with two or more faces, or with interchangeable heads. All were 'Victorian'.

Two of the most typical, and contrasting, Victorian dolls appear together in plate 33. The smaller wax-over-composition young lady, with stiff limbs and eyes that move only when the wire is pulled, was a popular doll at the beginning of Victoria's reign. The larger doll, a little girl with a bisque head, fully-jointed composition body and limbs and weighted eyes, was a favourite in the 1890s. The changes of style, composition and manufacture are clearly illustrated.

But, unfortunately for the doll historian, neither is marked with any trade mark or number by the makers, distributors or sellers.

According to the demand for them, dolls or dolls' heads made, for example, in 1900 might appear in the shops for a short period only, being superseded by new lines, or else continue to be made for twenty or thirty years if they continued to be best sellers. The Armand Marseilles baby and little girl dolls had long runs for bisque-headed dolls. London toy-shops were selling My Dream Babies more than ten years after their original creation: and little country shops, with a line or two of dolls in stock, might have had some 1901 Flora-dora dolls left on the stockroom shelves, thirty or more years later. Even as late as the 1960s a distributor's cache of Minerva tin dolls' heads, virtually as good as new, was discovered still in their original boxes.

Although it is not always easy to discover the actual period during which a particular line of dolls was in fact made, dolls with marks stamped or incised on their necks, shoulders and/or bodies do provide several clues.

A mark including the words 'made in . . .' indicates the doll was most probably made from about the turn of the century: the name of the country alone is an earlier mark, as from 1891 onwards dolls imported into this country had to be marked in some way with their country of origin. One Tradesmark Act was, in fact, passed in 1862, but dolls bearing this word seldom appear until the mid-1870s. The German 'Schutzmarke' or tradesmark was first used in 1875 but DEP (déposé or deponirt) was not used to indicate the date the doll's design was registered until 1884. Even so, it must be added that the doll as a whole cannot always be dated, even when clearly marked. Accidents will happen, also distributors find one line of heads hanging fire while

49

another sells out, and so it is perfectly possible for a doll to be sold to the public for the first time having a body of one date and the head of another. Thus the maker's name on a doll's head, even when the code number gives the date, will not always mean the doll's body is the same age, or even that it came from the same country; see p. 44. The little bisque doll sitting in a rather determined way on her chair in plate 32 has a head with the incised mark SH 4 above the number 905 at the back of the neck. This gives a probable date of 1888-90 and the formation of the letters is that used by Simon and Halbig. However the body may very well be French because several French doll companies imported the German Simon and Halbig heads and fitted them to bodies of their own making and dressing.

The porcelain-headed doll standing in a rather unladylike and equally determined posture beside her is older. The doll is unmarked but the composition and style, the fine quality of the moulding of face and hair, as well as the cut of the kid body, suggest it was made during the 1840s, possibly in Sonneberg, Germany.

The illustrations show how the high glaze of the 1840s dolls gave way to the more natural-looking, softer tints of the bisque favourite of the 1890s. Their wigs of real or mohair emphasised the delicate child-like appeal of these little girl and boy dolls. These dolls could all have been 'Sunday dolls', that is, treasures which were kept safely out of a child's reach all the week, owing to their cost and fragile heads, and which were brought out as a treat on Sunday for the little owner to hold when sitting quietly. If the family was a wealthy or indulgent one such dolls might possibly have been used for play; their status depended largely on the mother's opinion as to the most suitable toy for the strenuous everyday make-believe indulged in by most children of that time. It is known that the pensive-looking bisque-headed doll wearing a coral necklace was a real companion during the 1890s to the little girl who dressed and undressed her beloved 'Margaret' every day – and who nearly drove the maids frantic by insisting that her dolls' clothes were included in the weekly wash and returned to the nursery duly starched and ironed.

Margaret had been bought in Paris by Colonel Rees for his elder daughter. Disliking dolls, she quietly laid it aside and returned to her music, turning a blind eye to the 'rescue' of the doll by her younger sister, Sybil. In spite of the inordinate amount of attention she gave to Margaret the doll remained undamaged throughout Sybil's child-hood, and when her own daughter was old enough Margaret, restrung and redressed in her little bronze shoes and lace trimmed clothes, was given to her in the mid-1930s. Like mother, like daughter – Margaret was my cherished playmate for many years, which only goes to prove the fallacy of regarding bisque-headed dolls as too breakable to be good playthings. Certainly no modern doll ever endured more loving care, and one wonders if, forty years on, another contemporary child's daughter will want to play with her mother's plastic dolls and find them as undamaged as Margaret has remained to this day; see plate 33.

The immaculate condition of the beautiful wax-doll in plate 34 is less surprising. According to the provenance kindly provided by the former owner, it had always been kept, wrapped in tissue paper, lying on a bed of cotton wool – with extra little pads under its head, hands and feet – in a pasteboard box. Her mother, who had never been permitted to do more than look at such an exquisite treasure when she was a child, only allowed her daughter to see the doll out of its box as a rare privilege. Although the taffeta dress was removable, as were all the underclothes, it is doubtful if the costume was ever changed. The lace at the doll's wrists has been sewn across each hand to make a pair of mittens, and it has proved quite impossible to undress the doll without cutting the stitches.

Even though unmarked, as far as one can discover, it bears all the signs of being a Pierotti doll; the fine inset hair, the quality of the moulding of face, hands and high-arched feet speak for themselves. And the wax, still with the original bloom apparent on face and shoulders, is thin enough for light to be seen through the doll's head when it is held up sideways to a window-pane. In addition, the head appears to be identical to one owned by a member of this famous family, which is known to have been made about 1910.

The Pierotti family have the longest continuous history of com-mercial wax model and dollmaking in England. From 1780, when Dominico Pierotti, son of an Italian wine exporter, arrived in

England for medical treatment then unobtainable in Italy, to the retirement of Charles Ernest Pierotti, his great-grandson, in 1935, Pierotti dolls were made and sold continuously: a remarkable record, spanning some 155 years.

Dominico joined his uncle who lived in Portsmouth where he and his English wife had a business modelling papier mâché and plaster ceiling reliefs, as well as dolls and shop figures. But, like every other young Italian, Dominico headed for London just as soon as he was fit enough. Once in London he supported himself by modelling panels for interior decorating. But, around 1790, he turned to wax dollmaking, though not for lack of plaster work, since he was highly skilled and had made quite a name for himself in this field. One cannot help wondering why he made this change. Did his English aunt, the Portsmouth dollmaker, start this interest in doll-making by asking him to help her during his convalescence? Or had there been a branch of 'image-makers' on the original Pierotti family tree back in Italy? Certainly that country was renowned for such figures, as antique prints of Italian and English 'Street Cries' show.

Dominico's son, Enrico or Henry Pierotti, was also trained as a plaster moulder, and he, too, following in his father's footsteps, turned to full-time wax modelling. Although he made wax images and portraits, it was mainly for his beautiful child and baby dolls with poured-wax limbs and heads that he achieved fame.

Both the families of Montanari and Pierotti produced beautiful realistic baby dolls during the 1850s and 1860s; and both have been credited with the creation of this 'new' type of doll shown in plates 40 and 50. It is certainly true that Henry Pierotti claimed to have invented the 'Royal Baby' doll – a doll which might best be described as a portait model of whichever one of Queen Victoria's children happened to be current baby at the time. On his handbill, *c* 1860, is a verse describing his trinkets and toys. Two lines refer to dolls:

> Such beautiful dolls that will open their eyes,
> You may wash, comb and dress them and not fear their cries.

and, at the foot of the leaflet appear the words,

> observe the address –
> H. PIEROTTI, Inventor of the Royal Model Dolls
> Gallery, London Chrystal Palace, Oxford Street.

This 'Chrystal Palace' is, of course, the shop selling toys and fancy goods where Henry rented a gallery and sold his dolls, and not the famous Exhibition site. These shops so often had evocative and fascinating names. Which young customers would not want to visit 'The Beaming Nurse's' shop or 'The Dolls' Home'? Even though they might have hesitated to ask to be taken to 'Edlin's Rational Repository of Amusement and Instruction'!

When Henry died in 1871 the dollmaking business was carried on by one of his eight children, Charles William. But ill health, due to lead poisoning some six years later, forced Charles William to hand over the running of the Pierotti family business to one of his sons, Charles Ernest, who was helped by a younger brother, Henry. Charles Ernest continued dollmaking after his father's death in 1892, only retiring, at the age of 75, in 1935. Then, after four generations had worked for a span of some 155 years, the Pierotti family finally ceased to be dollmakers.

Bearing in mind the changes in doll designing since 1900, it is a remarkable tribute to their makers that Pierotti dolls were still being sold by such firms as Hamleys at least thirty years after the manufacture of wax dolls had virtually stopped everywhere else.

Talking recently to a niece of Charles Ernest Pierotti, it was fascinating to hear how, as a little girl, she had played a small part in the family saga. It seems that the widow of Charles William continued to make the bodies for the dolls in the house of her son, Charles Ernest, while Henry, his brother, made the wax parts and assembled the dolls in his own home. Whenever fresh supplies were needed, 'Uncle Henry' would call out to his niece, who lived there after her mother's death and ask her 'to run round to Granny's house for some more bodies'!

Somehow this homely touch seems entirely fitting, for these dolls were never the mass-produced products of some big impersonal factory. Each one was an individual character, created with something more than mere skill.

It is often well-nigh impossible to state categorically 'that doll is a Pierotti, that one a Montanari' if the doll in question is an unmarked child doll. However, as the one in plate 35 has several of the hallmarks of a true Montanari doll it may fairly be described as a Montanari type, even if it cannot actually be authenticated as a marked Montanari doll. The very short, thick neck and slightly sullen expression, the colouring and composition of the wax, the creased plump arms and the dark brown ringlets, all suggest Montanari. In general Pierotti dolls might be summed up as looking happier, their wax colouring usually pinker and with a softer, almost flesh-like quality and normally with flaxen or titian tinted hair (see plates 34 and 50).

Both firms made expensive dolls, which led to probably the only possible criticism of their work. Officials at the 1851 Crystal Palace Exhibition – the real Crystal Palace this time – complained that the dolls exhibited by Madame Augusta Montanari 'are adapted for children of the wealthy rather than for general sale. Undressed dolls sell from ten shillings [50p] to one hundred and five shillings [£5.25]. Dressed dolls are much more expensive.' Comparing these prices with the 1880 price list of 'general sale' dolls on page 178, and remembering that the value of money was much greater in 1851, there does seem to be a legitimate reason for making them Sunday best dolls. 'Crying dolls, wax, painted or comb, earrings, fancy painted boots, balance eyes 4/- [20p] *per dozen* . . . doll with dresses and clothing in a glass-top box 1/11 [just under 10p]: fine model boy or girl, wax head, wax limbs, *inserted hair*, 5/- [25p] each.' Even with the depreciated money of today how one longs for just a few hours in London, 1880. For the price of one modern plastic undressed doll it would be possible to equip an entire nursery with toys when Jack-in-the-box cost ninepence (4p) per dozen and a rocking-horse with glass eyes and a rocker 1½ m (4–5 ft) long could be had for about £1.

Compared with the saga of Pierotti wax dollmaking, the Montanari story is short, but their family history is still puzzling doll historians.

That seventh veil, hiding so many dates and relationships, has still to be removed if we are ever to know who all the dollmaking members of the family were, and in what relationship they stood to one another. However, some unquestionable facts are known. There were at least three and possibly four Montanaris who made dolls during the period c 1850–80. Napoleon Montanari exhibited wax figures and dolls at the 1851 Crystal Palace Exhibition and Augusta Montanari showed a display case of dolls, ranging from infants to adults arranged in an elaborate setting. She received a prize and much public admiration for this beautiful work.

It is not certain whether these two were brother and sister or sister-in-law, or husband and wife, nor where they came from before arriving in England. The name is Italian, but there is some reason to suppose they had come to England from the Americas. If so, it was perhaps from Mexico, as Napoleon was famous for his full-size wax figures of Mexican Indians, which were recorded as being modelled from life. It is also known that they exhibited dolls of wax and linen in the 1855 Paris Exposition. Both Napoleon and Augusta had several addresses in London over the years, and did not always share the same one. She died in 1864.

However, the main confusion about the family occurs over Richard and/or Richard Napoleon Montanari. Was he one and the same man, or an uncle and nephew? The dates of the Exhibition at which a 'Richard Montanari' is recorded as showing wax and rag (in this case wax-dipped muslin masks) dolls suggests that there might have been two men, as the 'Richard Napoleon' who was Napoleon's son and exhibited in the 1871 Exhibition, would seem to have been too young to have been the 'Richard Montanari' who displayed dolls at the Paris Exposition in 1855. None of these mysteries, fascinating as they are to doll historians, would have worried the fortunate children who were given Montanari dolls; the dolls themselves were enough to satisfy any child, no matter who made them.

Two of the most famous names in the field of bisque-headed dolls are Jumeau and Bru. Both are French, but the Jumeau company, founded by Pierre Francois Jumeau, pre-dates that of Bru by some twenty-four years and was one of the biggest dollmaking companie in the world. The actual date of its founding is uncertain, but in 1842 both Belton and Jumeau were listed as makers of dolls' bodie (the heads were imported from Germany). They also made an dressed their dolls in complete outfits. Indeed it is as a dolls' couturie that Pierre Jumeau – in 1847 a solo dollmaker but soon to be joine by a son, Emile – was first acclaimed. Jumeau dolls and their outfit won a Bronze Medal at the 1849 Paris Exposition and a prize Meda at the 1851 London Exhibition, although the judges there stated tha while 'the dolls on which these dresses are displayed present no poin worthy of commendation . . . the dresses themselves are ver beautiful.'

From then on, at International Fairs and Exhibitions all over th world, from the USA to New Zealand, the name of Jumeau wa prominent among the gold and silver medallists.

It seems a trifle odd now that the lovely Jumeau doll faces, so mucl admired and sought after today, were apparently ignored at thi time. Yet it must be remembered that, probably until the Franco Prussian war disrupted the import of doll heads, 'Jumeau dolls' di not necessarily mean dolls with Jumeau-made heads. Not until 187 did their advertisements specifically mention the dolls' heads speciall made for their dolls at their own factory at Montreuil. From then or the International Exhibition reports no longer comment on the dolls costumes alone, lovely though they were: 'M. Jumeau has establishe at Montreuil, near Paris, a factory where he makes doll heads o enameled porcelain [*sic*] with the greatest perfection . . . they [th judges] congratulated him on his beautiful product and awarded him unanimously the Medal of Progress.' At this 1873 Exhibition in Vienna Jumeau dolls also won a Gold medal.

In 1876 they were shown at the Philadelphia Exhibition. Again, the dolls' heads, as well as their superb clothes, are picked out fo comment, '. . . a fine collection dressed in the most fashionable style; heads of the finest imitation, superior taste and excellent workmanship in mechanical construction.'

Two years later the founder of the firm retired and Emile Jumeau went on to even greater successes, when Jumeau dolls were awarded the coveted Gold Medal at the Paris 1878 Exposition in competition with the products of other great dollmakers, such as Bru, Steiner and Schmitt. Their success continued. Melbourne, New Orleans, Antwerp and Paris . . . at all these Exhibitions during the next eight years Jumeau dolls were awarded Gold Medals and Diplomas of Honour.

At the beginning of the 1880s around 85,000 dolls were made annually at the Montreuil factory: by 1884 the number had risen to 220,000. By 1887 Jumeau was advertising that seventeen sizes of dolls' heads were in constant manufacture, and that 'six to seven hundred of each size are manufactured every day'. Jumeau was unusual in that the company now supplied all the necessary parts of the doll and its wardrobe: the heads, bodies and limbs, wigs and eyes, clothes, footwear, even the boxes they were packed in, not to mention the packing-cases for the boxes.

During the 1890s, when competition from the German firms was increasing, production of Jumeau dolls was boosted by the creation of a walking and talking bébé.

To further combat German competition Jumeau and several other famous French dollmaking firms amalgamated in 1899 to form the Société Française de Fabrication des Bébés et Jouets; see page 47.

There are two distinct types of Jumeau dolls, the beautiful childlike bébés of plate 36 and the smaller fashionably dressed poupées similar to the dolls in plates 41 and 42.

All Jumeau dolls which were sold dressed had exquisite costumes. These fashionable ladies could be bought with trunks and cases filled with every conceivable requirement from footwear to headgear, lorgnettes, gloves, parasols, fitted writing and dressing-cases, every item a perfect replica in miniature; see plate 41.

Just as there are similarities, as well as differences, between Pierotti and Montanari dolls so there are between Jumeau and Bru – as plates 36 and 37 show.

Of the two, the firm of Bru tended, perhaps, to be the more adventurous. Not only did they experiment with materials for some of their lines of dolls, such as rubber, 'hardened paste' and wood, as well as using the more general bisque with composition or kid bodies, but they included many novelty dolls, both 'mechanical' and those with coloured (oriental) faces.

Between 1867 and 1869 Leon Casimir Bru patented a crying doll and a two-faced 'surprise doll'. Madame Bru's 'surprise doll' of 1872 had a kind of musical box in its torso. Later, Casimir, Leon's son, applied for several patents for innovations, like the nursing Bru known as 'Bébé Teteur', some rubber dolls, and several improvements for eye mechanisms. In fact, by 1881, the firm had applied for twenty-one patents for dolls and doll parts.

Although the company name of Bru Jne et Cie was retained from 1883 until the SFBJ was formed in 1899, the firm was, during those years, run first by H. Chevrot in the 1880s and then by Paul Girard up to the time of the amalgamation. Under Chevrot several patents were added to the list, including a 'Bébé Dormeur' who joined the 'Bébé le Teteur' and 'Bébé Gourmand', still in production, in 1885. Paul Girard also added a few. Experiments with eye mechanisms continued, the famous 'Bébé Petit Pas', with its 'clockwork' mechanism, and various 'kissing' dolls and 'breathing' dolls were all patented by either Paul or Eugène Girard.

The Bru dolls were, of course, exhibited at the big international exhibitions which were so popular during the third and fourth quarters of the nineteenth century. At first the awards were silver; however, once M. Chevrot took over, the gold medals seemed to pour in with almost monotonous regularity: Paris and Antwerp in 1885; Liverpool and Paris, 1886; Le Havre and Toulouse, 1887; Barcelona, Melbourne and Paris in 1888. The silver medal awarded in 1889 must have come as rather a shock.

Needless to say, the firm of Bru was not the only dollmaking company to bring out new novelty dolls. Some years previously, in 1862, a doll had been patented in the USA by Joseph Lyon. This was the Autoperipatetikos, probably the best-known of all types of 'walking' doll. Dolls of this type, whether they had bisque, porcelain, papier mâché or composition heads, had a bell-shaped lower half with protruding metal feet set in lurching locomotion by winding up the mechanism hidden in the bell under the doll's skirt.

Many varieties were produced in the USA, Britain and Europe.

The one shown in plate 38 is unmarked on the head (which looks like a typical Steiner model) but has two labels, one underneath and one inside the hollow bell, with the words:

CHAS. MARSH
Wax and Composition Model Doll Manufacturers
114 Fulham Road S.W.
opposite the 'Queen's Elm'
DOLLS CLEANED AND REPAIRED

From 1865–94 Charles Marsh was one of the better English wax dollmakers and his wife, Mary Ann, was listed as a doll repairer from 1895 to 1910. Neither could have made this doll, so it must be presumed 'seller' should be added to the mention of 'repairer' and 'maker of wax and waxed papier mâché' dolls later in the advertisement.

This walking doll has a set of little wheels, not feet, under the bell; and the key, fixed into one of the two gaps cut in the canvas-covered cone, is low down on the left-hand side of the skirt. The rod, which also sticks out, acts as a kind of direction aid as it can be set to make the doll go forwards or revolve. When performing either movement its arms move slowly up and down – and have an unnerving habit of occasionally moving of their own volition. The doll is identical to a known Jules Nicholas Steiner doll. There is also another 'walking Steiner', but this doll has its mechanism, again worked by winding a key, fitted to its kid-covered torso and, when at rest, its properly made feet and legs make it look like an ordinary doll. The metal rods governing its movements are fixed inside its limbs.

In 1855 Jules Nicholas Steiner founded the firm, which was contemporaneous with that of Jumeau and Bru, and a rival of some merit. Under his direction Steiner dolls won many awards, gold medals and diplômes d'honneur. The firm also applied for several patents and produced many fine lines of dolls, walking and talking ones, as well as ordinary bisque-headed dolls with fair, negro or mulatto complexions. After Steiner's death the firm came under the direction of several men, and Madame Lafosse, the widow of one of them. In 1908 the firm ceased to be listed.

Another novelty doll was made in wax, composition and bisque. As well as having a mama-papa talking mechanism the one in plate 39 has two heads. This is the version patented by Fritz Bartenstein in the early 1880s. The face revolves by turning a ring on a rod going down through the doll's head into its cylindrical body, the stiff covered pasteboard bonnet hiding either the crying or smiling face from view. This is the type of doll that either immediately attracts or repels. In my experience most young children, especially the boys, automatically turn the faces round to see both expressions and then choose to leave the wretched doll twisted so that it has two noses where its ears should be, and an ear appearing in an otherwise blank 'face'. Other versions were made. One included a sleeping face if there were three faces to the revolving 'egg' within the doll's bonnet.

Novelty dolls of all kinds were popular – for a time: but the two best-sellers of the late nineteenth century were the English wax baby doll and the French bisque-headed fashion doll (plates 40 and 41). Both are expensively dressed and both were expensive dolls. The English wax doll, probably a Pierotti, has poured-wax head and limbs attached to its soft stuffed body by threads sewn through eyelet holes on to the fabric torso. The hair is inset, and the workmanship equals the appearance of this fashionably attired infant of the late Victorian age.

The elegantly costumed young lady on the opposite page has every reason to look so self-satisfied. In her trunk are her best scarlet corsets, several straw and silk hats, her umbrella – her parasol is on her arm – two fans and a fan case, bronze kid slippers and boots, silk stockings and handkerchiefs. The box for her beautiful muff rests at her feet, as do her blue enamelled brushes, comb and hand mirror. The cases contain all her other paraphernalia: writing equipment in the blue case, sewing implements in the red, and her manicure set in the small brown one.

It is believed that the first shop to cater solely for the needs of dolls like this opened in Paris shortly after the ending of the Crimean War in 1856. From then on dolls have never looked back. Even today's plastic platinum blondes are supplied with vital accessories, including boy friends and ponies, and to provide each doll with her own personally designed requirements would require a dress allowance of Victorian proportions. Famous designers, such as Mary Quant in England and Pierre Balmain in France, create specially for miniature clients. Mary Quant, admittedly, has designed several ready-to-wear outfits, but Balmain, realising, as a true Frenchman, that fashion is a serious business and that tiny stature should not preclude one from haute couture, has produced for his clients the fabrics and paper patterns from which the doll's own personal dressmaker may recreate a Balmain original.

But mock fur fabrics, PVC coats and boots, nylon stretch pants and tights, plastic hi-fis and transistors cannot achieve for modern dolls a semblance of the wonderful elegance of the truly sophisticated doll in plate 41. In those days, gracious living was not confined to a few fortunate Parisiennes. Dolls as far away as Massachusetts could be equally well provided with a Saratoga trunk full of beautiful things. One such doll appeared at a Boston Sanitary Fair in December 1863 with 'five dresses, a riding-habit, capes, cloaks, hats, shoes, slippers, bonnets, fur muff and tippet, reticule, undergarments, riding whip etc. etc.'.

The 'Sanitary Fair' may sound puzzling to people to the east of the Atlantic, where the word has a slightly different connotation. These fairs were originally sponsored by the Sanitary Commission to raise money for northern soldiers in the American Civil War, and, backed by some public-spirited people in Manhattan, they achieved their purpose. Doll exhibitions were always a feature of the Sanitary Fairs, which could probably best be compared with a Red Cross Fair today.

The elegance of the chiropodist's patient in plate 42 is not limited to her clothes, although her ensemble, with the charming little enamel watch pinned to her bodice and silver mesh purse, merit the closest attention. The whole construction of the doll's body, with its flexible ball-jointed limbs and delicately tinted bisque face, proclaims the high standard of the late nineteenth-century French doll designers. This doll is unmarked, but the one in the blue dress was made by F. Simonne, a Parisian dollmaker from 1847–78. Although there are

Simonne bébés and mechanical dolls, it is the bisque-headed fashionable ladies which are best-known.

Although the names of Bru, Jumeau, Steiner and their peers are justly famous, many beautiful dolls were designed by other makers, who remain unhonoured and unsung because their creations were made before it became obligatory to stamp them with a trade mark or maker's name.

In plate 43 are two coloured dolls, apparently having a slight altercation over a time-and-motion report. The mulatto doll brandishing a watch is marked with the initials FG, but the darker maid is without any identification marks at all. Both dolls have rather worn, coloured kid bodies and limbs, and both have curly black mohair wigs. This FG mark in itself often presents problems, as the dolls so incised might very well be made by Gesland or Gaultier (Gautier). It seems more likely in this instance that Gaultier is the maker; see page 42.

Coloured dolls were popular during the 1890s, and were certainly not confined to the 'little black baby' variety. The word elegant could be applied with as much right to the young girls with coffee or tea-coloured complexions as to their peaches-and-cream fair-skinned cousins (plates 28 and 29).

However confusing dolls' marks may sometimes be, the problem they offer to someone trying to discover their maker is as nothing compared to that presented by the great population of earlier unmarked dolls. The three dolls in plates 44 and 45 might very well be asking 'How should I remember? Us? *We* haven't a clue!', although in reality they were posed in this way to display their arms and hands.

Long before the fame of the English poured-wax dolls the country was renowned for two entirely contrasting dolls, one made of paper, the other of heavy wood.

The sixteenth- and seventeenth-century 'Bartholomew Babies', wooden dolls with carved features and clothes sold at the notorious London Fair, were the playthings of many children. But the heavy, carved, painted and jointed dolls, with their elaborate wigs and beautiful clothes, were the treasured possessions of comparatively few wealthy owners. One such doll is known to have featured in an

Englishwoman's will of 1548: the bequest was given on condition the doll was included with the estate to be handed down to the next generation, a condition which was maintained for nearly two hundred years.

The doll in plate 44 although of a similar type is an early nineteenth-century example wearing the clothes of 1825. This doll has a particularly well-carved head and body, gesso-coated and painted. The jointing of the limbs is unusually good, largely due to the use of rounded pegs. The wigs of dolls like this could vary from mere wisps of human hair glued or nailed on to the wooden head in a fringe under its cap, to properly constructed wigs, attached to a soft cotton skull cap fixed to the doll's head and dressed according to the latest fashion.

The dolls, being of the hand-carved bespoke kind, differed enormously according to the whim and skill of the dollmaker concerned. The early seventeenth-century ones had arms which were often little more than nailed-on strips of material between elbow and shoulder to join the spade-shaped, carved wooden hands to the body. Around 1700 the hands suddenly became much larger, and were often realistically carved with separate fingers and thumbs. Later hands might resemble the Chinese carved dolls with their elongated fingers of bamboo or wood, or the dolls might have arms and hands like the coloured, long kid-gloves worn by the wax-dolls at that time.

The eyes are interesting. The early blown-glass eyes had no pupils, and the iris was extremely dark, an almost black brown. Later, glass dolls' eyes, used mostly for bisque and wax-headed dolls, were exported in vast quantities from England in the 1850s and 60s. Birmingham firms made the majority but it was a Bristol paper-weight maker who made the beautiful type of glass eye, although French firms perfected the process in the 80s and 90s. However, these dolls' eyes were the flat-backed kind and not the bubble-shaped variety. Dating, and assessing the nationality of these dolls, can be a problem. The eyebrows and lashes sometimes give a clue, for the dotted line effect is generally regarded as typically Georgian. Although usually known as 'Queen Anne', these big, heavy wooden dolls could be more accurately described, if one must link them with the monarchy, as 'Georgian'. Certainly more Georgian dolls were made than Queen Anne ones, but, even so, this type of doll was first made long before the Hanoverian line reigned.

The high forehead design of the wooden doll is repeated in papier mâché for the pair in plate 45. Both kinds usually wore wigs, but the wooden heads were left plain, while the papier mâché heads had painted hair underneath, often with a 'feathering' of little curls across the brow. Both these dolls have inset dark brown eyes without pupils, and open mouths with tiny bamboo teeth. It is their bodies that differ so greatly from one another: the bigger doll has a soft fabric body, with kid, long glove type arms, but the smaller has a beautifully shaped and stitched kid body, and limbs of the same kid with V-shaped joints at the elbows, hips and knees.

According to Charlotte M. Yonge a papier mâché-headed doll with a white leather body could be regarded as a novelty doll during her childhood in the late 1820s and early 1830s. This is interesting because the dolls illustrated were probably made during this period and are of a type widely exported from Sonneberg at that time. Indeed, since the discovery, c 1810, that papier mâché was an ideal material for mass-produced dolls, they had been exported in increasing numbers.

The best-known of all the Sonneberg papier mâché dolls were the kind known as 'milliners' models', from their often extremely elaborate and fashionably moulded hairstyles. The taller, standing doll in plate 46 is the typical milliners' model. Like her companion, she was probably made during the late 1820s or 1830s. The hairstyles of both were popular in high society in the early 1820s, but it would take a little time for the styles to come into general favour and in country districts they would still be fashionable well into the 1830s. Although this style of doll is often referred to as a 'Queen Adelaide' it is not a true likeness of Princess Victoria's aunt-by-marriage. It is – if one dare use the word 'merely' when describing the elaborate hairstyle – merely the fashion associated with that Queen. The doll's body is made of tightly stuffed white kid, and her lower arms and legs are of carved wood, with the well-known little bands of coloured paper covering the joins. Pretty though her dress is, it is a pity one

1. A Sakura-ningyō (cherry doll), typical of the decorative display dolls so often seen in Japanese homes — hence its popular name 'shelf doll'. She represents the Warrior's Handmaiden in a Kabuki drama and has a stiffened fabric face mask and is built up on a padded wire framework. Height: 35 cm. (14 in.).

2. Two Hina-ningyō (Festival Dolls). These Dairi-bina, or Exalted Personages, represent th
Japanese Emperor and Empress in the annual ceremonial display on 3rd March, the Festiv
for girls or Ohina-matsuri. The dolls have gofun covered heads and the Empress wears th
traditional Chinese style Imperial Crown. Height (seated): 15 cm. (6 in.).

3. Another Hina-ningyō, this time from a display for Tango-no-Sekku, the annual Boys' Festival on 5th May. This doll represents the legendary giant, Benkei, waiting at the Gojō Bridge armed with his Seven Weapons — axe, saw, naginata, rake, sodegarami and sword. Height: 22 cm. (9 in.).

4. A typical English Pedlar doll, an old woman in a red cloak and a black bonnet with a tray of wares. This particular doll represents an old pedlar woman who used to sell her wares in London's Threadneedle Street in 1870. Height: 25 cm. (10 in.).

5. 'Henrietta', a rare, 19th-century version of an English Pedlar doll in that she is young and beautiful. The delicate, realistic modelling in wax of face and hands, the carefully braided hairstyle, are unusually fine for this type of doll. Height: 25 cm. (10 in.).

6. An early Victorian 'conversation piece'. This homemade room setting, with its example of industrious Young Ladies usefully occupied with their needlework under the watchful eyes of their preceptress, is a good model of a typical amateur English ornamental display. The dolls, with their tiny yellow hair-combs, are all little pegged-wooden ones, probably from the Grödner Tal. The room is approximately 45 cm. (18 in.) wide.

7. A French automaton, c. 1880s. Musicians were popular subjects for automata, as the dolls could be made to 'play' the tune produced by the hidden musical-box. This young mandolin player's body, with its mechanical movements, is metal and pasteboard, but his hands and head, marked F. G., are fine quality bisque. The eyes are blown glass and the wig is mohair. Height: Approx. 76 cm. (2 ft. 6 in.).

8. A Fortune Teller, made in Germany, probably in the mid 19th-century. This rare example of a black wax doll has a 'pumpkin' head, and eyes of pupil-less inset glass. The fortunes are hand-written on the folded pleats of her paper petticoat hidden under the skirt of her home-made dress. Height: 30 cm. (12 in.).

9. Russian dolls with Chinese ancestors. The Matryushkas are brightly coloured wooden 'nest' dolls which pull apart to reveal smaller dolls within. The biggest one here contains only five dolls, but some have as many as 25 or more. Height: 15 cm. (6 in.). The little balalaika player is a daruma-type doll, weighted so that it cannot be knocked over.

10. Kokeshi, the traditional wooden folk dolls made in north-east Japan since the early 17th-century. Originally makers, while using their own designs for ornamentation, kept to the basic 'ninepin' shape of the tallest kokeshi at the back: more modern examples show the variations of shape and design, and the use of fabrics added to the wood. Heights: 5 cm.-25 cm. (2 in.-10 in.).

11. Cheap 19th-century wooden dolls made in the Tyrol. They were then sent to Holland and exported from Dutch ports by local merchants, hence their name 'Dutch dolls'. The smaller group are earlier and better made, the bigger dolls show clearly the later crude carving and and pegging of the joints. Height: 3 cm.-45 cm. (1½ in.-18 in.).

12. *Above (left to right)* North American homemade dolls: Indian woman with a corncob body; farmer's wife and baby, 'shuck' dolls from cornhusks; schoolmarm with a wooden body and hickory nut head; 'Johnny Appleseed' with a dried apple head and limbs of chicken bones. Heights: 17 cm.-25 cm. (7 in.-10 in.). *Below (left to right)* Central and South American folk dolls: straw musician from Central America; lichen-dyed raffia man and horse from Mexico; varnished leather pedlar from Peru; palmetto fibre doll made by the Seminole Indians of Florida. Heights: 10 cm.-25 cm. (4 in.-10 in.).

Right Eskimo doll, representing the son of a 'chief', made entirely from fur and skins with embroidered features. This is the full winter costume. The smaller doll is Russian and is made of beaten flax fibre and wood. *Below* Czechoslovakia cornhusk dolls, made from the natural undyed husks.

14. *Above* Modern examples of traditional paper dolls. The natural looking Scot is made of crepe paper over a wire frame. The two flat Japanese Anesama-ningyō are of printed papers folded into shape. The peasant girl shows the fine detail of her native Poland's art of cut paperwork, even the stripes are separate strips of paper. Heights: 12 cm.-22 cm. (5 in.-9 in.). *Below* The Japanese lady is a 'stick' doll. Her body is just a stick or wire with the fabric clothing carefully cut and positioned to achieve the most natural effect. The two European printed pasteboard cut-outs have been padded with cotton wool before the fabrics and trimmings were added. Heights: 12 cm.-17 cm. (5 in.-7 in.).

15. *Above (left to right)* The two English books of *Moral Tales,* about 'Little Henry' and 'Little Fanny' with paper dolls and cut-out costumes, were published by S & J Fuller in 1810. The early 20th-century examples, from the 'Dollyland' box, were produced by Raphael Tuck. *Below* These pages of early English 19th-century fashion dolls, with hand-coloured costumes show the development of the idea towards the later mass-produced brightly printed examples in plate.

WELSH DOLL

These are the Welsh names for her costume:

HAT, black beaver—HET

Frilly white MOB-CAP—BONET

SHAWL, made of plaid flannel — SIÔL

Detachable SLEEVES,
—LLEWYS.

Myfanwy Jones in her best dress

DIRECTIONS
Cut along the dotted lines around front and back views. Pin the two together, printed sides facing, and sew along the printed edge. Do not sew the bottom of the skirt A–B. Nick the edge at the angles of neck, hat, and waist for better shaping.

APRON—FFEDOG

OVERGOWN—BETGWN

PETTICOAT—made of striped Welsh flannel—PAIS

Turn Myfanwy right out and stuff her kapok or soft rags, push the stuffing down into the hat, head and arms. Fold in edges at A–B oversew them tog...

6. *Above left* The American Raggedy Anne dolls, from his book about the character, were patented by Johnny Gruelles in 1915. The little red-headed rag doll in Raggedy Anne's arms is 19th-century Bulgarian. The two pressed rag dolls by her chair are Russian, from a set showing costumes from all the regions in the USSR. Heights: 8 cm. (3½ in.) high; Raggedy Anne, 55 cm. (22½ in.). *Below left* Sheets of printed rag dolls, ready to be cut out and stuffed at home, are as popular now as they were in the 1890s, when hundreds of designs were printed in England and the USA by such firms as Dean's Rag Co. and the Arnold Print Works. This is a modern Welsh example.

7. This is the 1955 mass-produced version of a doll originally designed by Kathe Kruse in 1910. Disliking the stiff commercial products of that day, and inspired by her sculptor husband, she first experimented with a potato and a cloth, trying to produce a doll which looked and handled like a baby, so that her children could have a true play doll. Height: 25 cm. (10 in.)

18. General 'Chinese' Gordon mounted on his horse. The model rider and his steed were first
     carved and then covered with two layers of material before being painted. They were made
     in India in 1900 for the son of the Scottish Chief Engineer on the Bengal and NW Railway
     Height: 58 cm. (23 in.).

La Parisienne

19. Contemporary dolls in traditional costumes from the UAR. The gossiping group of an Egyptian cotton-picker, a snake charmer and Arab bystander and the one woman listener, have painted limbs and features. The more unusual guide is all fabric, with embroidered features. 'La Parisienne' herself, the creation of an old dollmaker from Esneh, is also of fabric, with tin sequin ornamentation. Heights: 15 cm.-30 cm. (6 in.-12 in.).

20. 'Unbreakable' tin and celluloid-headed dolls were the 1890s equivalent of the modern vinyl plastic variety. The standing doll with a jointed composition body has a Minerva tin head made by the German firm of Vischer. The head of the larger seated doll is celluloid and made by Rheinische Gummi und Celluloid Fabrik Co. Her jointed wooden arms fit onto a kid body and legs. The small doll has a Minerva tin head and shoulderpiece, composition arms and calico body. Heights: 45 cm. (18 in.), 76 cm. (30 in.), 30 cm. (12 in.).

1. The 1920s softer type of unbreakable doll. Christopher Robin is a felt Italian Lenci doll. Nanny, who also has a pressed felt head, has velvet arms and was made by the English firm of Chad Valley. Piglet, and the invisible Small on his back, are English also, 1950s copies of the toys made for the original Christopher Robin. Heights: 45 cm. (18 in.), 40 cm. (16 in.), 17 cm. (7 in.).

22. Litle all-bisques . . . save for the elevated black-haired bath doll. She has a glazed front and unglazed stoneware back to enable her to float in the bathwater. The jointed ceramic toddle in a knitted outfit is, like the seated baby, probably a Heubach doll, though marked only with the letters DEP — registered. The Kewpie doll, also German, is marked O'NEILL on the feet. Heights: 12 cm. (5 in.), 11 cm. (4½ in.), 13 cm. (5½ in.), 16 cm. (6½ in.).

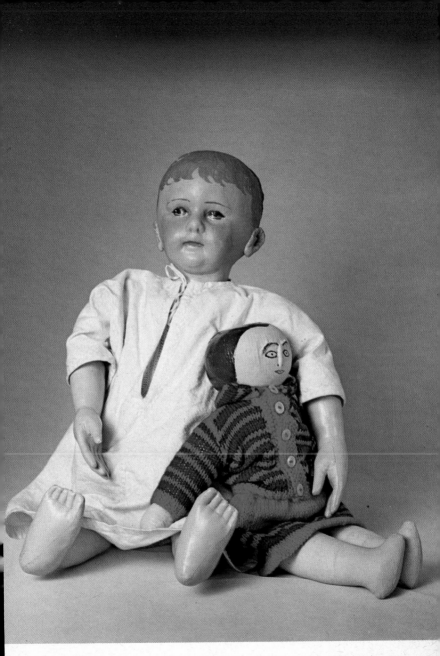

23. Two heavyweights. The big boy still wears the gown of St Thomas's Hospital, London, one of the many hospitals throughout the world to use these American Chase stockinet dolls in nurses' training. He evolved from the original 1890s play dolls designed by Martha Chase. The smaller, though extremely heavy, is still a play doll. Its two designers made the first Cobo dolls in Guernsey in the 1880s. Heights: 60 cm. (24 in.), 30 cm. (12 in.).

24. Three early-mid 19th-century wax dolls. The biggest has a wax-over-composition head and shoulders and wire operated eyes, *c.* 1820s. The standing doll has a poured wax head, with inset hair and fixed eyes, *c.* 1850s. The seated one has a late 'pumpkin' head of wax-over-composition, moulded hair with an Alice band and weighted eyes, *c.* 1860s. Her hands and feet are of wood. Heights: 68 cm. (27 in.), 45 cm. (18 in.), 45 cm. (18 in.).

25. These two turn-of-the-century babies illustrate vividly the changing styles of dollmaking and provide a complete contrast to the earlier wax dolls. The doll in blue is German, made by Kley and Hahn; the other is French, made by the Société Francaise de Fabrication des Jouets (SFBJ). Both have bisque heads and jointed composition bodies. Heights: approx. 35 cm. (14 in.), 45 cm. (18 in.).

26. A group of late 19th- and early 20th-century dolls, showing the growing popularity of dolls in national costume. The Dutch boy, *c.* 1930, is German-made by H. Zwanzger, the face is stiffened, painted calico. The Scottish boy, also most likely of German make *c.* 1890s, has a composition head and lambswool wig. The Peasant Girl, with bisque head and hands, is French. Her mark, FG, probably denotes F. Gaultier, 1860s-1916. Heights: 35 cm. (14 in.), 25 cm. (10 in.), 35 cm. (14 in.).

27. The dolls in this group have the additional attraction of ethnic as well as costume appeal. The aristocratic Chinese, with traditionally long fingers, was made for export, the head and limbs are painted wood. The little black boy, of fully joined papier mâché with fixed pupil-less eyes, still has a working squeaker, exactly 120 years after it was given to little Miss Glaisque. The Japanese baby is a modern *yamato-ningyo* with traditional costume and rattle. Heights: 25 cm. (10 in.), 22 cm. (9 in.), 25 cm. (10 in.).

28/29. Some of the ethnic dolls made in Europe, which became increasingly popular from the late 1880s. Simon and Halbig, the German firm, brought out their coloured bisque-headed dolls with fully jointed composition bodies during the 1890s, advertising them as 'The Dolls of Four Races'. Both the European and Indian dolls in these photographs have 'flirting eyes' i.e.

mechanism moving the eyes sideways as well as up and down, a design credited to the same dollmaking firm. The Oriental doll, although also marked 'SH' was made by another German firm, Shoenau and Hoffmeister. Heights: 45 cm. (18 in.), 30 cm. (12 in.), 12 cm. (5 in.), and 6 cm. (2½ in.).

30. Armand Marseilles, 'My Dream Baby' was a universal favourite for years. This German-made best-seller, first produced in the 1920s, has a bisque head with weighted sleepy eyes and a jointed composition body. The firm also made a coloured version; both dolls were produced in sizes ranging from a few inches to life-size. Height: 50 cm. (20 in.).

31. From the Dream to Reality. The American 'Byelo Baby' in the chair, modelled from life by Grace Putnam in 1922, became such a best-seller in the USA it was known as 'The Million Dollar Baby'. The other baby, also with a more 'natural' bisque face, has a jointed composition body not a soft one, and is German marked FBT inspired by the Kammer & Reinhardt 'Baby' of 1909. Both approximately 31 cm. (12½ in.).

32. China and bisque examples of these two popular ceramic types. The German doll with a glazed china head and hair and its stiff-limbed kid body is *c.* 1840s. The Simon & Halbig doll, *c.* 1888-90, has an unglazed bisque head and hands, inset sleeping eyes, mohair wig and jointed kid body which contribute to the more natural look favoured in later decades. Heights: 38 cm. (15 in.) and 30 cm. (12 in.).

3. Early and late 19th-century favourites: two unmarked dolls showing the great change in doll design. The early wax-over-composition doll has a hair wig, wire-operated eyes and a soft body. 'Margaret', the late bisque-headed doll, has a mohair wig, weighted glass eyes, and a jointed wooden body. Heights: 43 cm. (17 in.) and 55 cm. (22 in.).

34. Pierotti . . . a beautiful example of wax-dollmaking, unmarked, but probably by Pierotti. The head, with blue glass eyes and inset blonde mohair, hands and feet are of thin poured wax: the body is stuffed with cow's hair. Strictly a 'Sunday doll', she was only admired lying in her box and was never played with either by the first owner or her daughter. Height: 40 cm. (16 in.).

35. and Montanari . . . the second of the two most famous wax dollmakers. Another unmarked doll, but with the classic Montanari features. The wax is thicker and less pink than most Pierottis, the expression less happy, the eyes set more pensively, the inset hair darker and the workmanship is of the same fine quality. Height: 66 cm. (26 in.).

36. Two more 'rivals' . . . First, the French firm of Jumeau, famous and most prolific manufacturers of the quality bisque-headed dolls in the 19th-century. This typical Jumeau bébé has the later paperweight eyes, a mohair wig, and a body of jointed composition, with relatively large hands and feet. The Jumeau factory made the whole doll, its clothes — even the packing cases — an unusual feature and, by 1887, produced 700 dolls' heads in 17 sizes each day. Height: approx. 71 cm. (28 in.).

7. Bru . . . from the 1860s rivalling Jumeau until their merger with other firms to form SFBJ (Société Francaise de Fabrication des Bébés et Jouets) in 1889. Both examples shown have closed mouths, fixed glass eyes, pierced ears and mohair wigs. This Bru doll has their characteristic heavy eyebrows and delicate bisque lower arms: the head swivels on bisque shoulders set on a jointed kid covered wooden body. Height: 50 cm. (20 in.).

38. Novelty dolls were popular in Victorian times: this example *c.* 1870s is one of many Walking Dolls. The bisque arms move up and down as the doll moves forward or in a circle; the clockwork mechanism is hidden in its lower bell-shaped stiffened canvas half which bears the label of Charles Marsh, 114 Fulham Road. The head, probably by Steiner, is bisque, with deep blue fixed glass eyes. Height: 38 cm. (15 in.).

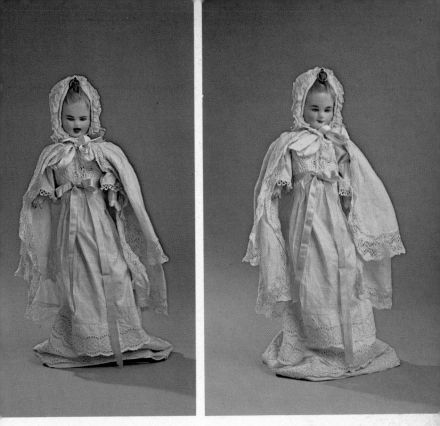

39. Another novelty was the multi-faced doll, its 'reserve' faces being hidden by its stiffened canvas bonnet fixed to the body. This one has only two faces, smiling and crying; but some had a third, sleeping, or were multi-racial — or even characters like Red Riding Hood and the Wolf. A German doll made by Bartenstein c. 1880s, has a wax head, turned by the ring on a canvas-covered cylindrical body; the limbs are jointed composition. Height: 40 cm. (16 in.).

40. A typical mid-Victorian English wax 'baby' doll, dressed to full panoply of a fashionable infant of the period. The stuffed cotton body has, however, straight 'adult' legs: the feet and arms are poured wax, as is the shoulders and head-piece. The doll has dark brown glass eyes and inset blonde mohair. Height: 66 cm. (26 in.).

41. And a typical French 'Fashion' doll: bisque hands and head, swivelling on a bisque shoulder-piece, inset glass eyes, mohair wig and fully jointed composition body. Each exquisitely made miniature accessory is a perfect replica of the full-size article. This fortunate doll's trunk includes enamelled toilet set, parasols, underwear, etc, also cases of sewing items, writing things, manicure set, fans and muffs. Height: 43 cm. (17 in.).

42. Two fine examples of French adult poupées-bébé being, naturally, the name for the child-doll only. Both have delicately coloured bisque heads, mohair wigs and fully jointed bodies, the seated dolls' body being particularly flexible owing to the wooden ball joints. She is unmarked, the standing doll with bisque hands is by F. Simonne, 1847-78. Height: approx. 45 cm. (18 in.).

43. Fashions alter — but not domestic problems. The fine mulatto doll is marked FG (probably for Gautier) the darker one is unmarked. Both have bisque heads, glass eyes, mohair wigs and jointed dark kid bodies, the FG has pierced ears. Black dolls were much favoured in the 1890s, elegant adults generally pre-dating true baby dolls. Heights: approx. 40 cm.-45 cm. (16 in.-18 in.).

44. The more unusual type of early 19th-century English wooden doll has an almost Egyptian profile and pose. The big glass inset eyes are pupil-less, the wig real hair and the body very well jointed with round pegs. After carving the wood was coated with gesso and painted. Note the long fingers of these realistic hands. Height: approx. 55 cm. (22 in.).

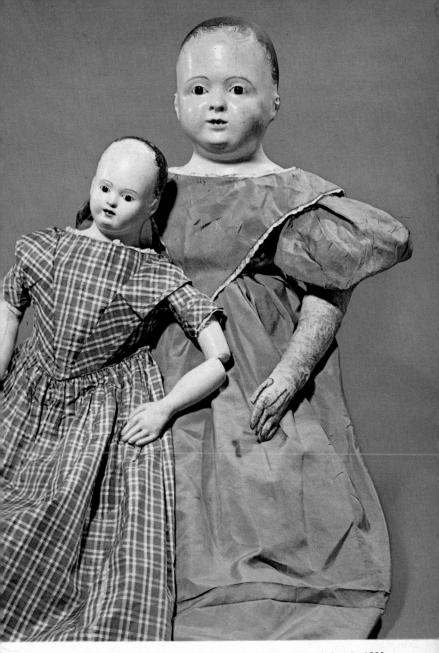

5. Two papier mâché dolls heads, of the type mass produced at Sonneberg during the 1820s-1830s, shown here without their additional mohair wigs. Their inset glass eyes are pupil-less, their mouths open with four little bamboo teeth. The smaller dolls' body is very fine being well jointed and stuffed pale pink kid, the other doll has a rather shapeless cotton body and kid arms. Heights: 66/50 cm. (26/20 in.)

46. Two more 1820s-1830s dolls in complete contrast to the previous pair. Now usually described as 'milliners models' because of their fashionably ornate moulded hairstyles. The taller has a papier mâché head, kid body and wooden arms and legs, and is a typical example. The seated doll is unusual, being made entirely of wood, well jointed at hips, knees, elbows and shoulders. Heights: approx. 38 cm. (15 in.) and 25 cm. (10 in.).

47. Sonneberg, already famous for wood, papier mâché and wax dolls, began exporting porcelain headed dolls *c.* 1840. These two dolls have porcelain lower arms and legs and jointed wooden bodies. Note the seated doll's hairstyle, reminiscent of the young Queen Victoria's, and the hole through the right fist of her companion. Heights: approx. 30 cm. (12 in.).

48 *Above* Two superb examples of porcelain dolls' heads, made in Sonneburg during the first half of the 19th-century. The moulding of both is particularly fine, and the hair colouring of the one on the left is unusual. Heights: approx. 7 cm.-10 cm. (3 in.-4 in.). *Lower* From the sublime to — 'Dorothy', as the incised mark shows, is an English ceramic head, made in Staffordshire *c.* 1920s. Height: 15 cm. (6 in.).

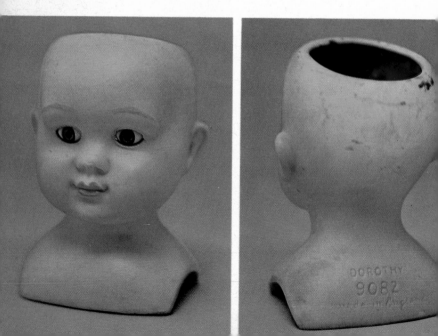

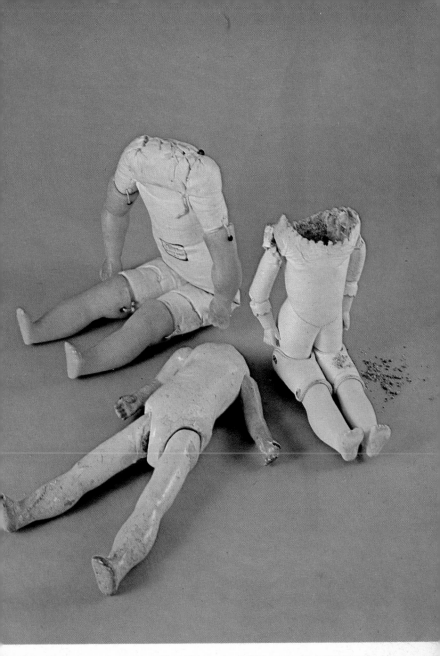

9. Three of the most common types of late 19th- and early 20th-century dolls' bodies. *(Back to front)* The body of an English Lucy Peck wax doll, *c.* 1900. Jointed sawdust stuffed kid body for a French or German bisque head, shoulders and lower arms and composition legs. Cheap composition jointed body for a socket-type bisque headed doll, this example was a French SFBJ. Heights: 25 cm.-40 cm. (10 in.-16 in.)

50. The Nanny, c. 1900, has a wax over composition head, a mouth painted to show two rows of teeth and an abundant auburn wig. She and the baby are exquisitely dressed in handmade clothes. 'Jack', the boy twin, has, like his sister (not shown), a stuffed body with poured wax head – inset with mohair – and limbs. They are marked 'F. Aldis . . .' and are thus probably by Pierotti as Aldis used these heads. Heights: 43 cm. (17 in) and 25 cm. (10 in.).

51   Two bisque dolls of the parian type, probably German, *c* 1850-70. During the 1860s dolls
with fashionably moulded hairstyles and hats with a lustre finish were very popular. 'Mama's'
boots are the pre-60s flat-heeled kind, her 'son's' are later, having tiny heels. Note the different
arm lengths – fashion seems to have altered more vital lengths than hems. Heights: 25 cm.
(10 in.) and 17 cm. (7 in.).

52. An unusual composition-headed and limbed doll with the helmet moulded onto its head. Unfortunately its history is unknown, but it may be a commemorative doll as it has been dressed in the uniform of a Rifle Corps Volunteer *c.* 1860, and was later presented to its local museum at Colchester, Essex. Height: approx. 25 cm. (10 in.).

53. A more usual type of commemorative doll, dressed to represent Queen Victoria, has the porcelain head and limbs which were so familiar during the mid-19th-century; but an expert needlewoman has dressed it in this beautiful replica of one of the Queen's dresses. Height: approx. 20 cms. (8 in).

54. World War I had prevented the USA importing bisque doll heads from Germany. To overcome the shortage the Fulper Pottery Company, New Jersey, made 21 lines during 1918-21. This one is from a range of 'little girl' socket heads with wigs and inset glass eyes. Height: 55 cm. (22 in.).

55. Dolls made in the Staffordshire Potteries after imports from Germany stopped during World War I. *(Back to front)* 'Dorothy, 40, made in England', socket-head, fixed glass eyes, open mouth with teeth, wig. A Hewitt Brothers (Willow Pottery) shoulder head, painted features. Another Willow shoulder-headed doll, ceramic limbs, painted hair and features. Unmarked felspar head and limbs, fixed glass eyes, moulded hair, long cork-stuffed body. Heights: 45 cm. (18 in.), 35 cm. (14 in.), 38 cm. (15 in.) and 53 cm. (21 in.).

56. Two generations of Israeli newsboys. The smaller original wire-and-fabric doll was made and sold to aid Jewish refugees in the 1950s. The bigger one, with modelled head and limbs, is produced by the Wizo Home Industries, to show different Israeli characters. Heights: 12 cm. (5 in.) and 20 cm. (8 in.).

57. Chinese farmer and wife. Modern 'rag' dolls designed by Ada Lum and made in her Hong Kong workshops. The dolls, of stuffed cotton with embroidered features, wear authentic replicas of traditional costumes. The farmer wears everyday garments, and his wife her best embroidered indoor shoes and headscarf. Height: 45 cm. (18 in.).

58. 'Harry the Hawk', the parachutist designed by Norah Wellings and sold in aid of the RAF Benevolent Fund during World War II, is of pressed felt with painted features. The civilians below are French, handmade during the Occupation of France from oak apples, old kid gloves and scraps. Heights: 17 cm. (7 in.) and 12 cm. (8 in.).

59. A *yamato-ningyo,* one of Japan's 'Silent Envoys'. Originally made as gifts for royalty to present to honoured guests, these dolls were later also sent as goodwill gifts to the children of other nations by the children of Japan. Height: 66 cm. (26 in.).

60. A modern 'rag' doll with a black wool wig, made in Hong Kong under the aegis of the Lutheran World Service and exported to raise funds for the mission. The doll wears a traditional Chinese brocade costume and has other outfits for different occasions in her wardrobe. Height: 35 cm. (14 in.).

A Yao Tribeswoman

1. Two fine examples of modern craftwork. The African doll, with her intricate beadwork costume, was made in the South African Red Cross Rehabilitation centre, Durban. The Yao tribeswoman from northern Thailand in her authentic garments was designed by Mrs Tongkorn Chandavimol and made in her Bangkok studio. Heights: 33 cm. (13 in.) and 25 cm. (10 in.).

62. An early 19th-century English wooden doll, with a painted, gesso-covered face, inset pupil-less glass eyes and crudely jointed limbs. She is dressed as a nurse at Colchester Hospital when it opened in 1821, and probably commemorates the event. Height: 30 cm. (12 in.).

63. Five more Colchester residents: this rather stiff and pathetic looking group of small wooden dolls, again with painted, gesso-covered faces, were dressed by a Mrs William Mason who lived there in the 1840s. They wear the uniform of the local Blue Coat Schools of that time. Height: approx. 25 cm. (10 in.).

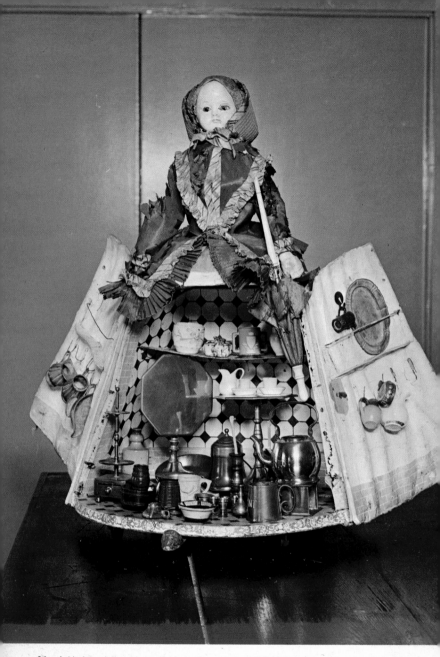

64. A kitchen doll made probably in Germany *c.* 1840. Off duty her hinged bell-shaped 'skirt' closes to hide the kitchen inside, transforming her into a pretty display doll, dressed in silk with a matching parasol. She was designed as a dual-purpose toy, to be both instructional and ornamental. Height: approx. 30 cm. (12 in.).

65. Doll's house dolls 1800-1900. *(Centre front)* Three hollow wax dolls *c.* 1800; *(right front)* a well-made fully jointed wooden one; behind her are 2 of the cheaper, cruder type. *(Left front)* A doll of the middle period with papier mâché head, kid body and wooden limbs. *(Middle row)* China-headed dolls, black-haired then blonde, with stuffed bodies. *(Back row)* Late nineteenth century bisque headed dolls. Heights: 5 cm.-13 cm. (2 in.-5 in.).

66. *Left* Pincushion dolls: this Victorian English version has a doll's body to the waist, her 'skirt' being a sawdust-filled pincushion and her apron a flannel strip for holding pins. Height: 17 cm. (7 in.). *Below* Japanese versions based on ejiko and kokeshi dolls. The kokeshi has a pincushion hat and tape measure 'feet'. Heights: 7 cm. (3 in.) and 11 cm. (4½ in.).

57. Basically the same, these bisque-headed dolls with lustre finished head-dresses show the different ways two individual Victorians chose to make them into 'Worktable Companions'. Just two pincushion pockets holding needles on one; but the other has pincushion hat, pockets for needles, bags for thimble and scissors, sash for thread etc. Height: 21 cm. (8½ in.).

68. Nanny . . . has a composition shoulder head, arms and lower legs and a soft body. Her eyes are glass sleeping, her wig mohair. The Winged Angel mark with *'Fabrik-Mark deponit'* stamped on the right leg is that of Stephan Schilling, registered in Germany in 1895. The doll was costumed in England in 1904 in a miniature replica of the dresser's uniform. Height: 60 cm. (24 in.).

59. Shoki the legendary Chinese 'Chaser of Devils'. His images were once believed to ward off illness by superstitious Japanese, who always had Shōki on display at the *Tango-no-sekku* (Boys' Festival) to protect their sons. Shōki has delicately painted gofun-covered head and hands and elaborate robes. Height: 55 cm. (22 in.).

70. Advertising dolls: 'Sunny Jim' a cut-out rag doll made originally as a sales promoter for 'Force' cereal, c. 1905. The design is based on the character created by M. M. Hanff. A 'Campbell Kid' first made in the USA c. 1900 by Horsman under licence of Joseph Campbell Co. Heights: 43 cm. (17 in.) and 30 cm. (12 in.).

71. American Personality Dolls. *(Left to right)* The aviator, Amy Johnson, a painted, composition-headed doll with soft body and limbs, dressed in a felt flying suit. Shirley Temple, a 1960s plastic version with moving eyes and washable hair, dressed as the heroine of the film *Rebecca of Sunnybrook Farm.* Madame Alexander's painted composition dolls representing the Dionne Quins as babies, made in the mid-1930s. Heights: 30 cm. (12 in.), 25 cm. (10 in.) and 15 cm. (6 in.).

72. Modern versions of old folk-dolls. *(Left to right)* Australian aborigine witch-doctor, made of wire and painted crêpe paper with a wool and feather head-dress. Unusual female version of a Japanese Daruma doll: these tilting dolls, named after the Indian Buddhist priest Dharma are usually male. Polish 'Tartar king', a painted wooden toy version of the hero of Kraków annual pageant of Lajkonik. Heights: 16 cm.-7 cm. (6½ in.-3 in.).

73. Variations on a theme in wooden dolls representing nuns. *(Right to left)* The Grödner Tal peg-jointed doll was dressed in England *c.* 1900. Egyptian Coptic patriarch and nun, *c.* 1970, show an interesting link with the Japanese Kokeshis. An early 20th-century kokeshi, given to an English visitor by one of the Japanese Royal Family. A modern kokeshi, made for export to France. Heights: 17 cm.-30 cm. (7 in.-12 in.).

74. *Above* A band of angels: woven raffia trumpeters from Ecuador, two Scandinavians of straw, a tiny maize husk Czechoslovakian playing cymbals and a French wax Infant Jesus. Heights: 17 cm.-5 cm. (7 in.-2 in.). *Below* Traditional English corn dollies: modern Cambridgeshire umbrella, ancient fan design from the Welsh borders, a Suffolk horseshoe and a harvest bell from the eastern counties. Heights: 30 cm.-15 cm. (12 in.-6 in.).

75. *Left* Corn maidens were made from the last of the harvested corn in honour of the fertility goddess. This one, from Montenegro, is made of oats. Height: 76 cm. (30 in.). *Right* The propitiation of the harvest or fertility goddess was universal, this plaited palm maiden was made in Bali. Height: 45 cm. (18 in.).

76. The Hopi Kachina doll, carved from cottonwood and painted to represent a god of the Pueblo indians, comes from the south-east USA. Totems were one way the Indians used to record their tribal identity. This one is typical of those from the northern regions. Heights: 17 cm. (7 in.) and 12 cm. (5 in.).

77. A unique set of Pierotti wax dolls, with glass eyes and inset hair, beards and eyebrows, made *c.* 1860s. Dressed in the robes of a High Priest, Common Priest and Levite of the Exodus period, they were used by John Whyberd (1847-1923) in his lectures on the symbolism of the Old Testament and its fulfillment in the New. Height: approx. 50 cm. (20 in.).

78. A modern Polish doll with painted composition head and hands, taw wig and soft body. He is carrying the traditional Schopa (Christmas crib) which accompanied the carol singers as they made their rounds on Christmas Eve. The miniature Schopa is of elaborately painted wood, but it can also be a simple box-like stable. Doll's height: 30 cm. (12 in.).

9. Figures from cribs or Christmas crêches made in Italy during the 18th-century. Many materials were used by the different crib-makers; this Madonna is from a set of padded wire figures with natural-looking wax heads, St Joseph has a head and hands of painted carved wood, and the King's head and hands are painted papier mâché. Heights: 17 cm.-20 cm. (7 in.-8 in.).

80. Traditional sugar dolls, brightly coloured with additional paper decorations, still sold in Egyptian streets on the feast day of the birth of the Prophet Mahomet. These are *Ariges-el Mouled* (dolls of the Birthday) for little girls, boys have little sugar horses and riders called *Halawet Mousa* (sweets of Moses). Height: 22 cm. (9 in.).

cannot see her dainty ankles and feet in their orange-painted, flat-heeled slippers.

Less typical is the smaller doll seated in a chair – and looking as if, by refusing to see the giantess beside her, she hoped it would Go Away. As well as a stiff upper lip she has a ramrod posture, but this, it must be admitted is due to the fact that from her head to her hips she is carved from a single piece of wood. The arms and legs, jointed at the elbows and knees are also of carved, rounded wood; altogether a more unusual body for this type of papier mâché head than that of the kid-and-wood giantess.

During the 1840s Sonneberg, already world famous for its wood, wax and papier-mâché dolls, added porcelain to the list. This great dollmaking region, one of the world's biggest centres, was renowned as far back as 1700 for the wooden dolls which the Grödner Tal turners sent there to be painted and distributed. Around 1800–10 the mass-production of papier-mâché dolls began. By the 1850s, the wooden, wax, papier mâché and porcelain dolls were being exported all over the world from various factories in the area. In 1903 it is recorded that twenty million bisque and china doll heads alone were manufactured by Sonneberg firms each year.

The doll holding her bonnet in plate 47 was most probably made in Sonneberg during the late 1830s. The articulated wooden body is rather crude, but the moulding and painting of the porcelain features and hair, together with the charmingly delicate clothes, make the whole effect quite delightful. The doll's right hand is interesting. It is curved into a fist, with a hole bored through the clenched fingers. It has been suggested that the doll was meant to represent Queen Victoria at her coronation, and that the hole was intended for the sceptre. Another theory is that this type of limb was universally used for 'Worktable Companions' (see plate 67) so that the doll might hold the bodkin. This doll, very sensibly, allows the speculation to rage over her untroubled head, since she uses the hole in her hand to hold her bonnet strings, so that the delicate article does not fall on to the floor.

The seated doll's hairstyle was a favourite of Queen Victoria during her young days in the 1840s. This doll was most probably made in

Sonneberg too, although, of course, it was not the only place famous for porcelain dolls. Some beautiful porcelain heads were made by such factories as the Königliche Porzellan Manufaktur, whose Berlin doll heads were particularly fine during the 1840s. Another famous porcelain factory was that of Copenhagen. Their doll heads, made mostly between 1840–80, had rich dark brown hairstyles, a striking contrast to the customary black. Again, the modelling and quality of these heads is noteworthy.

Meissen also produced a few dolls' heads; but they are rare indeed, 'Dresden' being far more famous for its exquisite porcelain figurines. It is almost as difficult to find a flaxen-haired porcelain doll as it is to discover a parian doll with raven tresses. However, the Meissen works produced one or two notable exceptions to this general rule.

Plate 48 shows clearly in close-up the superb quality of some of the 1840s dolls' heads. The head on the left has a most elaborate hairstyle, in a rather unusual shade for a Sonneberg doll, and a face with, again, an unusually animated expression.

The blue-eyed beauty on the right has a hair-ornament of exceptionally beautiful coloured flowers placed just over her ear. Another painted spray, of different design, is placed on the other side of the flat, plaited bun of her hair. The delicate tints of both these fine heads make them rare treasures indeed.

Coming down to earth abruptly, one may look at another head of almost equal rarity, although any other similarity would be hard to find between this rather comical little face and the goddesses above – no wonder their gaze is averted from the example so far beneath them! Nevertheless, the mark 'Dorothy' indicates she belongs to that little band of doll heads produced in the Staffordshire potteries (see page 152) and now so sought after by collectors. But, if one remembers Shakespeare's question: 'What's in a name?' the answer in this instance would have to be 'quite a lot'. For without it Dorothy would hardly merit at place, especially if she had been the product of some French or German factory. Nevertheless, as a weekday play-doll Dorothy had her merits, but the two photographs vividly illustrate the difference in the makers' approach to the art of ceramic doll-making.

A head without a body, when it is of the standard, so to speak, of the two top people in plate 48 may be of ornamental interest in itself, but it is not much use as a doll. Some of the later nineteenth-century dolls' bodies in general use are shown in plate 49. The cotton body, stuffed with the cows' hair that indicates it was made before kapok and similar fillings became popular, has wax limbs, attached by threads sewn through eyelets sunk in the wax – the style most frequently used by the makers of poured-wax dolls. This actual body has a purple inked stamp showing it was made for a wax Lucy Peck doll:

FROM
MRS PECK
THE DOLL'S HOUSE
131, REGENT STREET
— W —

Lucy Peck, like the Pierotti family, was one of the rare wax dollmakers whose dolls were still popular in England as late as 1921. From the marks on Peck dolls it seems that her shop, where she sold and repaired all kinds of dolls as well as making wax ones, had several moves. Some of her earlier dolls, made around the turn of the century, still had a wire to pull and push to open and close the eyes. Others had fixed, flat-backed or bubble-shaped blown glass eyes sunk in the wax sockets. Most of her dolls had inset hair, often of fine human quality. From the dolls still to be seen today she seems to have used all kinds and colours of wax. Unlike the earlier Santy dolls, which were wax-over-composition, Lucy Peck used the poured-wax method for her dolls.

Herbert Meech, another famous wax dollmaker of the 1860–90 period, seems to have used both methods for his dolls, and he also had the distinction of being 'by appointment' dollmaker to the Royal Family.

The cheap-looking, jointed composition body spreadeagled across the foreground seems an unlikely component part of an SFBJ doll, but such is the case. Very often the big doll manufacturers used cheap, rather crude, bodies for their lower-priced range of dolls, although the bisque heads fitted on to them were of far better quality. This inexpensive type of doll frequently had only two joints, at the shoulders and hips, even though such dolls were made at the same time as the fully articulated kind, which had ball joints at elbows, wrists, knees and ankles.

The white kid body, stuffed with sawdust, has bisque hands and composition lower legs and feet. It is the kind which usually supports a bisque shoulder-head, the scalloped neck edging of the kid being stuck over the bisque bust. It was the interim stage between the body completely made of white or pink kid, and the wholly composition ball-jointed kind.

The body of the Nanny doll in plate 50 is made of straw-stuffed, glazed cotton; the lower arms are composition, as are the legs in their painted mustard-coloured high-buttoned boots and white stockings. The shoulder head is wax-over-composition with a very pretty light auburn mohair wig. This doll was given, in 1903, to a little girl who for some inexplicable reason christened it 'Nurse Cross'. This was a curiously inappropriate name, for the doll's face is very pretty, with a half-smiling mouth, painted to show a row of tiny pearl-like teeth. However, the child certainly disliked the Nanny although, like Doctor Fell, 'the reason why she could not tell'. But the two baby dolls which came with the Nanny were very much loved.

Nanny's costume is of particular interest as it is not only beautifully made but is an authentic miniature replica of a contemporary uniform. The attractive little blue velvet hat, with its ivory ruched silk lining and long floating veil of thinnest silk, is firmly attached by tiny hat-pins with blue glass heads to the doll's hair and to the organdie 'strings' which tie under her chin. A voluminous silk poplin cape covers a pale blue cotton bodice and skirt and a belt of dark blue to match the cape covers the white apron's waist-band. Underneath the fine cotton, lace-trimmed waist petticoat is a pair of lace-trimmed drawers, worn over the matching lace-edged lawn chemise. The doll's most fascinating garment is the one, unfortunately, which is never seen. Her candy-striped pink and white corsets are lace trimmed, and have matching pink 'stay laces' through the rows of eyelet holes at the back. The front is hooked together to give the doll, in spite of all her layers of clothing, a very trim figure.

The poured-wax baby on her lap is a twin; the pair are not identical as this one, 'Jack', has flaxen inset hair while 'Jill' is a brunette. Both have blue eyes, a healthy pink complexion and are exactly the same size. The outer robes differ slightly although both dolls' outfits are exquisitely handmade. Jill does not have the cape and her robe is of the finest lace-trimmed lawn, her bonnet ribbons are pink and her bib's lace trimming matches that on the bonnet.

Although so faint as to be almost unreadable her body is stamped with what appears to be the mark of F. Aldis of 11 (?) Belgrave Mansions. Frederic Aldis was a London maker and importer of dolls, who is known to have used the wax heads made by Pierotti on some of his doll bodies. The twins certainly seem to have all the attributes of Pierotti dolls: the texture and colour of the wax, the type of blue eyes, the beautifully shaped inset hairstyles and the moulding of both faces and limbs are all instantly recognisable.

Jack's white cape and bonnet are made of fine spotted muslin, with blue ribbon and lace trimmings. His robe, with tiny rows of insertion and lace trimming, goes over a plainer under-robe of matching fine lawn, also lace-trimmed. Under that is a long wrapper of fine nun's veiling, ribbon edged. A bodice lining of finest lace-trimmed lawn acts as a vest. Round his body is wrapped the typically Edwardian baby's flannel binder.

The elegant doll on the opposite page is a parian doll, probably made in Germany *c* 1850–70, although it might have been made in England. These dolls often seem to have arms of a length more suited to an ape, but the feet, shod in dainty little flat-heeled ankle-boots, could not be more ladylike. Her hat, on top of a beautifully moulded coiffure, is particularly noteworthy. During the early 1860s there was a vogue for this type of parian doll, wearing a delicately tinted hat trimmed with a feather of a lustre finish; see plate 51.

The little boy gives the impression that he, also, is only too aware that his fashionable little high-heeled boots are too small for him. It is not too heartless, I hope, to reflect with some amusement how often one sees just this same pained expression on the faces, not of

149

dolls, but 'guys' nowadays . . . truly, *il faut suffrir pour être beau*! The doll is unmarked, as is his mama, but is probably German, made in the late 1860s or 1870s.

The slightly older doll in plate 52 also appears – in spite of the rigour of a military life – to have, so to speak, a head too big for his boots. The doll's body is firmly stuffed coarse muslin and the limbs are composition, as is the interesting head with its moulded plumed helmet. The doll is dressed in the uniform of a Volunteer in the Rifle Corps *c*. 1860. As it was given to a local museum, the unit was probably an Essex one. The excellent condition of this doll, 110 years after its making, suggests that it was not a true weekday play-doll, but rather a special doll to be admired on a Sunday afternoon.

There was a phase, about this time, when commercially made and dressed military dolls were very popular. But, fortunately for the social and regional historian, the amateur recorder has always tended to use dolls when seeking to commemorate special occasions and events, and it is to the makers and dressers of these dolls that we are indebted for much information that would otherwise have been unknown. Naturally, not all the characters chosen for commemoration were local people. National characters have been chosen by such famous dollmakers as Pierotti and Montanari, whose General Lord Roberts and elderly Queen Victoria, made at the time of the Diamond Jubilee in 1897, are such outstanding examples of wax portraiture.

But, equally, it was not only the famous manufacturers who made records of people and events. The portrait doll of the young Queen Victoria in plate 53 is a commercially-made porcelain doll, but the beautifully sewn and embroidered dress was made at home by a dedicated needlewoman. Once again the condition of the doll and its costume clearly illustrate the care with which it has been kept over so many years.

Although this tradition of making commemorative dolls is still maintained, one cannot help wondering, rather sadly, how many of the commercial 'Queen in her Coronation robes', 'Beatles', and 'Cosmonauts' will be kept so carefully by – and to some degree, from – the younger generation today. And, even more sadly, how many of the dolls are worthy of such care?

5

Dolls at Work:
Teachers, promoters
and recorders

As I sat in a room in Park Lane in 1954, holding two smiling, obviously homemade rag dolls dressed in brightly coloured clothes, it was difficult to realise that 'Odette' had made them in a Nazi prison during the war. No one, unaware of their story, could possibly guess the suffering associated with those two little dolls.

No child, looking at the dolls in the group on plate 55, would see them as anything more than attractive playthings: yet, although their personal histories are not as harrowing as that of Odette's dolls, each owes its creation to some crisis or problem.

As World War I had stopped the import of bisque doll heads from Germany into the USA, the Fulper Pottery Company came to the American doll manufacturers' aid in the years 1918–21. The firm had been established in New Jersey since 1805 but, until the crisis produced by the war, had not considered the manufacture of commercial bisque doll heads. However, under the direction of J. M. Strangl, the chief ceramic engineer who designed the dolls, a production line of 22 different doll heads, in many sizes, was achieved by 1921, the third and final year of the company's dollmaking activities. During those three years the Fulper Pottery made doll heads for such doll body manufacturers as Amberg and Horsman. With some pride, they boasted that their doll heads were completely American, made from American ingredients in an American pottery. But the resumption of imports from Germany in 1921 ended the endeavour, as they could not compete with the output from German factories; see plate 54.

Naturally, World War I had ended the export of German dolls to

England also. Here it was the Staffordshire potteries who, at the instigation of the Board of Trade, tried to make good the loss. Unfortunately, through inexperience and manpower shortage, the quality of the dolls they made in no way matched that of the more traditional Staffordshire products. Probably because of this – and also because the dollmaking venture was seldom more than a short-term sideline – few records were kept, and the potteries concerned have always been reticent about their achievements in this line. Staffordshire dolls are comparatively rare, and what little is known about their production is largely due to the personal reminiscences of ex-potters.

W. H. Goss of Stoke-on-Trent, better known for the souvenir Goss Chinaware, probably produced some of the best dolls, but their prices were high and, once Germany started exporting dolls again after the war, they were forced out of this market by a flood of cheaper and better-made German imports. At firms like the Mayer and Sherratt China Manufactory at Longton, the Empire Porcelain Company, the Willow Pottery and the Cauldon Works, dolls had an equally short span. Only a very few potteries, notably the Blue John Factory and Diamond Tile Company, kept up the dollmaking sideline and went on producing a limited quantity of dolls right up to World War II.

After the creation of the state of Israel, dollmakers there produced a series of little character figures. Each one represented a costume or occupation, either traditional or modern, illustrating a typical aspect of Jewish life. At first they were handmade, and were used to represent Israel at the popular exhibitions and displays of dolls under the auspices of the United Nations. Later they were manufactured commercially; and it is interesting to see how the little homemade newspaper seller, brought back from Israel in the 1950s, developed into the bigger character doll marketed by Wizo Home Industries as the 'Yemenite Paper Boy'; see plate 55.

While the Israeli dolls commemorate the founding of a nation, the two Chinese dolls recall a lost homeland. In 1939 Ada Lum, their creator, sheltered in her home many war refugees, some of whom had actually collapsed in the garden of her house in Shanghai. To muse the children she made dolls for them, copying their costumes, footwear and hairstyles so that they might have the extra comfort of familiarity; see plate 57.

Miss Lum, who visited England in 1957, told me that when she in turn became a refugee and fled to Hong Kong in 1948, she managed to bring her own set of dolls with her. There she set up a cottage industry, with the dual purpose of recording rural Chinese costumes and providing work for some of the thousands of refugees pouring into Hong Kong from mainland China. A staff of girls helped to make and dress the dolls in Miss Lum's home, but the traditional seagrass footwear, coolie blue costumes and straw hats, were made by refugee craftsmen and women scattered throughout the colony.

War again forms part of the background of the making of the dolls in plate 58. Norah Wellings – the English dollmaker famous for the little velvet and cloth mascot type 'Sailor Boys' and 'Darkies' – created 'Harry the Hawk' during World War II. Each little parachutist bears a circular RAF label with, on one side, the inscription 'Made by Norah Wellings. By arrangement with the Royal Air Force Comforts Committee an agreed percentage of the manufacturer's sales of these RAF mascot dolls is contributed to the Royal Air Force Comforts Fund.' On the reverse side is printed a picture of the doll, and its registered design number; round the outer rim of the circular label are the words ' "Harry the Hawk" Royal Air Force Comforts Fund'.

A unique pair of dolls look up to Harry in plate 58, much as their real-life counterparts may have done during the Occupation of France in the last war. They are two from a set of dolls made by an old lady who lived in a small village in the country near Paris. It distressed her that the local children should go without dolls at Christmas time, and so she began the task of finding scraps of materials for a series of little character dolls, probably based on the inhabitants of the village. The dolls had heads of painted oak-apples, bodies of cut-up worn kid gloves and they were dressed in any old pieces of cloth that could be spared. Odd though the little creatures may look, they were loved and carefully cherished by the children who received them from this 'Mama Nöelle'.

153

The exquisite Japanese doll appears to have little connection with the French oak-apples, but she, too, was designed to be a gift. In 1927, eleven thousand dolls were sent from the USA to Japan by the Committee of World Friendship among Children 'to take part in the Doll Festival' (Ohina-matsuri). In return 'the children of Japan' sent some of their 'Silent Envoys' to the United States, following their country's ancient custom of honouring friends and acquaintances with gifts of dolls. Yamato-ningyō, see also p. 43, created around the turn of the century and designed to represent children of that era, were the type of doll chosen for this particular mission of friendship.

Church missions have relieved suffering in many distant lands. Often, having given the vital medical aid, their most successful long-term plans have included as much handicraft instruction as religious and other teaching. The Lutheran World Service, Hong Kong branch, is no exception. Dolls like the one in plate 60 have been sent all over the world, proudly bearing white and gold woven labels proclaiming them to be 'Hand made in Hong Kong, for the Lutheran World Service Crafts'. This particular doll, 'Little Sister', travelled in the cane case with a wardrobe of five outfits, suitable (so the accompanying leaflet informed us in German) for Festival days, going to visit friends, everyday wear and so on. The bag she carries everywhere contains her lucky charm.

The African doll with the beautifully beaded costume also carries an identifying label pinned to her skirt. On one side it reads 'The South African Red Cross Society, Durban. This is a product of the Red Cross Rehabilitation Centre. We thank you for purchasing it, and hope that you and your friends will continue to support us.' The reverse side states 'Name of Doll . . . "Nomayeza" . . . "Herbs" '.

The story of the creation of the Bangkok Dolls, who conceal a very worth-while purpose under their beauty, is an interesting blend of inspiration and practical application. A few years ago Mme Tongkorn Chandavimol, accompanying her husband on an official cultural tour of Japan, was fascinated by the art of Japanese doll-making, particularly of the *sakura-ningyō* (literally, gorgeously coloured dolls). On her return to Bangkok she began designing dolls to represent not only the legendary characters of Thailand as porrayed in the country's classical dance dramas, but also the hill tribes of the north, the farmers and fruit vendors, and a series of men and women dolls showing the evolution of Thai costume. There is also a set of soft and cuddly dolls for children, but, like the model dolls, dressed with meticulous attention to the authenticity of their costumes.

Mme Tongkorn Chandavimol recently told me of her interest in the less affluent northern hill tribes, and how she had involved them in the making of her dolls. Some women of the Yao tribe slowly embroider their complicated traditional patterns on pieces of the black cloth used to dress the dolls representing the women of their tribe. Not only does the work provide much needed income, it also preserves an art form that was in danger of being lost. The actual pattern on the Yao Tribeswoman Doll in plate 61 is of particular interest. Another recent guest, who studies Balkan embroidery, told me that this pattern is a favourite in Bulgaria where, so it is said, the design has been used for centuries having been introduced by traders from the Far East – in fact from the Yao tribal region in north Thailand.

The exceptionally high standard of workmanship, and the authenticity of the design, lift both the South African and the Thai doll well above any souvenir classification. Such dolls fulfil the dual purpose of providing much-needed work for the makers and authentic records of previous cultures for the historians.

Two more 'research aids', of an earlier date, record the founding of local charitable concerns, plates 62 and 63, and show the costumes of that time. The Georgian wooden doll appeared as a miniature replica of a nurse in the Colchester Hospital, which was opened in 1821. The rather sad and solemn little group of wooden dolls on the same page were dressed by another Colchester resident, Mrs William Mason, c. 1840. The two little boys' attire might pass unnoticed today, but surely the little girls' would at once remind us of an orphan child of Victorian times. However, both costumes were worn by children attending the Blue Coat Schools in Colchester at the time the dolls were dressed, probably c. 1830–40.

The idea of 'Look-and-Learn' as a teaching method is probably, in one form or another, as old as the hills. The usefulness of dolls in this type of education is so well recognised today that authorities in Britain, and elsewhere, commission doll designers to make examples specially for schools. For many years doll exhibitions have been popular means of benefiting charities, promoting interest in and cultural exchanges between countries and commemorating events. But education, like so many other things, begins at home and, unless it was the Japanese mother of past years, nobody could equal the English Victorian mama when it came to making the best use of her children's possessions and leisure.

Starting with dolls' usefulness at home, upstairs, so to speak, are the Japanese *hina-ningyō*, downstairs the European Kitchen Dolls.

Toy kitchens of all kinds are still to be found, but the Kitchen doll, made during the nineteenth century, is rare. In one sense she could be described as an upstairs and downstairs doll, for, with her skirt ribbons neatly tied, she would grace any drawing-room cabinet in her silk dress, trimmed bonnet and parasol. But, as the children were admiring her beauty, Mama would swiftly untie those ribbons and reveal the true purpose of the doll – the cupboard of miniature pots and pans hidden so demurely beneath the doll's skirts – and a lesson on the proper use of the equipment in real life would begin; see plate 64.

Germany produced a somewhat similar doll in the 1840s. A painted wooden figure of a nun or monk would, at a turn of its waist, reveal a small three-dimensional triptych, complete with little carved praying figures at the altar and in the pews of the unsuspected 'church'.

Conscientious Victorian mothers could make subtle use of many children's toys as teaching aids. A painted wooden Noah's Ark was the highlight of many hours of Bible study, although its usual complement of highly unlikely-looking animals can hardly have aided the study of natural history. Pollocks' Toy Theatres, with their accompanying sheets of 'penny-plain' characters, were ideal for memory training and manual dexterity. 'Fashion dolls' aided dress-sense, and dolls of all kinds were used to model the results of the hours of needlework many little girls endured. And what better or more pleasant way to teach the fundamentals of housewifery to a child who would one day have to supervise the smooth running of her own household, than by using a dolls' house and its inhabitants? Cooks and parlour-maids, butlers and footmen all had their allotted rôles to play, and woe betide the little girl who expected her mother to accept the 'tweeny's' presence in the drawing-room of the dolls' house!

In elegant eighteenth-century 'baby houses', the wax family above stairs and the wooden staff below imitated everyday life in the child's home. Later, in the boxlike mass-produced late Victorian dolls' houses, little china-headed penny dolls and farthing wooden ones enacted their parts. The little group in plate 65 are some of the most popular types made during the nineteenth century. Around 1800 fragile hollow wax dolls were the tenants (A). These were succeeded by the delicate little pegged woodens with tiny yellow combs on their black painted hair (B) and then the less well-made, crudely painted 'Dutch dolls', the Mary-Annes (C). These, in turn, became the servants as the dolls with more natural-looking papier-mâché heads (D) took possession of the houses around the second quarter of the century.

In the third quarter came the china-headed dolls – first with black (E) then with blonde hair (F) – which were followed by the little bisque ones (G). These dolls often had beautifully moulded hairstyles and painted footwear, reflecting fairly recent if not actually contemporary fashions. A vogue for little bisque dolls with hair-wigs followed during the 1870s, but, from the late 1880s to the early 1900s the most popular dolls' house dolls seem to have been once again those with moulded hairstyles, which, of course, reflected the changing fashions in women's hairdressing. Again following adult fashion, the male dolls now sported very dashing moustaches (H).

Naturally few houses would be filled with only one kind of doll. Indeed, as Charles Dickens reminds us in *The Cricket on the Hearth* (1845), there was a distinct social hierarchy in the doll world: doll ladies and gentlemen were wax, the middle classes leather and the common folk wood. One wonders where he would have placed the wool-and-wire, felt, celluloid, bakelite and plastic dolls of today.

The little wax dolls of the late eighteenth and early nineteenth centuries are so fragile it seems miraculous that any survived more than 150 minutes, let alone years. So thin is the wax that it seems to have been blown rather than poured into a mould. Only the disproportionate size of their enormous feet, in coloured red or green 'shoes', keeps them standing. Even so, a breath would blow them over and as playthings they certainly had their limitations.

Far more practical in the child's game of make-believe were the little 'penny-woodens', although the splinter-like pegs which jointed those of dolls' house size must have been responsible for many lost doll limbs and tears of childish frustration. The popular name of these little dolls is quite misleading: a penny would buy four little crudely-made Victorian wooden dolls of dolls' house size, or two of 12.7 to 15.2 cm (5 to 6 in).

Frances Low, in her original article published in the *Strand Magazine* in 1892 disparagingly refers to Queen Victoria's favourite playthings as being 'common twopenny [1p] Dutch dolls', describing them as 'of the most uncompromising material . . . not aesthetically beautiful with their Dutch doll – not Dutch-type of face'. She adds acidly, 'they would be regarded with scorn by the average Board School child of today whose toys, thanks to modern philanthropists, are of the most extravagant and expensive description'. Whatever surprising light this throws on 'the average Board School child', to say nothing of the 'modern philanthropists', it is an almost libellous description of the delicate aristocrats of Dutch dolldom so beloved by the young Princess. For one single representative a child would have to give two whole pence (slightly under 1p), two weeks' pocket money and a sum large enough to procure eight Mary-Annes, the real 'common' little Dutch dolls. But even the twopenny nobility were frail, with easily dislocated limbs, and most children probably regarded the papier mâché or china-headed dolls as far more satisfactory dolls' house residents. Not only were their faces and limbs more realistic, but their sawdust-stuffed little kid or muslin bodies were much easier to dress.

What better inducement could there be for a young dressmaker to ply her needle and thread than to give her a 'Work-table Companion' and a pincushion doll? Since so much time was spent by the Victorian young in what adults regarded as suitably fitting occupations, it is hardly surprising that the heyday of both these dolls occurred during the later nineteenth century.

In fact the pincushion doll's history goes back much farther than this. There is a delightful illustration in an English book, *Pins and Pincushions* published in 1911, which shows a wooden doll, 60.9 cm (2 ft) high, charmingly and fashionably dressed, but with an additional pincushion petticoat and another pincushion as a kind of apron. The doll was given to three-year old Mariana Davis in Paris during the year 1747, when the little girl was recovering from an illness. It is to be hoped that the poor invalid was allowed to play with her gift, for even with a well-disciplined infant of the 1740s, the thought of a convalescence consisting of hours of plain sewing must surely have induced a relapse.

Pincushions are necessities wherever women sew, so it is hardly surprising to find another kind of pincushion doll in Japan. From their design the two circular ones would seem to be based on *Ejiko*, a doll representing a baby wrapped in a warm cover and placed in a straw basket while the mother worked in the fields.

The standing kokeshi version has the pincushion as his little circular hat, and this doll also contains a tape measure; see plate 66.

The English doll, also wearing a pincushion hat and carrying as well as a tape measure, packets of needles, thread, scissors, a thimble and a bodkin, is the kind known as a 'Worktable Companion'. This was a very popular Victorian doll and, although it could be bought in London as a fully made-up 'Companion', several magazines here and in the USA brought out their own designs and gave instructions on how to make an ordinary doll into one. Possibly the best-known version was one designed specially for *The Englishwoman's Domestic Magazine* in 1864, which wears the then fashionable red skirt with black bands. In the USA the March issue of *Godey's Magazine* that year offered its readers a pattern for a gipsy pincushion doll.

Some of the china-headed pincushion and companion dolls had curiously shaped right hands, clenched like a fist but with a hole through the fingers. Most probably the hole was designed to hold a bodkin, but some believe wool or silk was threaded through it to stop it becoming entangled while working; see also plate 47.

Many dolls of all descriptions were fitted out as Companions by simply tying the scissors on to a ribbon sash, and adding pockets to the dress to hold needles, thread, thimble and so on. According to the whim and skill of the adaptor, the finished result could be as simple as the first doll or as elaborate as the second in plate 67; both dolls were basically identical before their transformation.

The more ordinary pincushion doll is, strictly speaking, half doll, half pincushion, as the legs were either removed, the pincushion hiding the deficiency, or they were buried in the sawdust stuffing when the pincushion was being made.

Almost any kind of material, such as wood, celluloid, china, bisque, bakelite or plastic was used for the later types of pincushion doll, which continued to be manufactured throughout the first half of this century. But by then the doll-part was a true 'half-doll', with a hollow head and torso, made with holes along a low waist-line so that it could be sewn more easily on to a pincushion skirt. These half-dolls were also used during the twenties and thirties on clothes-brushes, hat-stands, powder-puffs, and larger versions appeared on night-dress cases. For a time there was even a vogue for covering the telephone with a 'Crinoline lady'. As the room also contained a Boudoir Doll, a long-legged wire-framed doll designed to represent a modern woman, usually wearing a fancy-dress type of costume, which would recline gracefully on a bed or sofa, a fully equipped bedroom could surely only have been suitably illustrated in a *Punch* cartoon.

At first glance the dolls in plates 68 and 69 do not seem to have much in common, nor do they appear to be particularly useful. But each in its own individual way, and in a manner characteristic of each country, represents with complete accuracy, a typical and highly respected national character. The English, of course, are responsible for the hand-that-rocked-the-cradle; the other powerful ruler of the children's world is Japanese.

Nanny's blonde hair suggests her teutonic origins, and this composition-headed doll was made by the German firm of Stephan Schilling *c.* 1900. But, on her arrival in England, she was immediately clothed in a replica of the dresser's own uniform and given to her little charge in 1904. It is of particular interest to costume researchers because the uniform confirms the fact that the flat white cap with two wide lace-trimmed lappets, the sleeve protectors and the metal chatelaine with its penknife and scissors, were still everyday wear for at least some English nannies in 1904. Under her blue dress are layers of petticoats, and her black stockings are kept up by long elastic suspenders from her dashing green-and-white striped stays (corsets). Her drawers and shift are of thin white cotton. The provenance of the doll was given by the doll's former owner, the little girl for whom nanny had dressed the doll seventy years ago. In spite of her kindly mien one feels Nanny would not tolerate any real naughtiness in her nurseries, and there is a similar firmness of expression about the Japanese figure. Exquisitely polite disdain seems to emanate from his very eyebrows, and there is no doubt that he could curb any juvenile tantrum if the occasion arose.

This doll most probably represents Shōki, 'the devil chaser', a character renowned in legend and also credited with the power to keep illness away from the recipient. Apart from this obvious reason for his popularity as a gift for children, the figure of Shōki is one of the two legendary heroes which are displayed at the Tango-no-Sekku. The other is Kintoki, who is usually represented as a child wrestling with a bear or riding on a carp, reminders of two of his legendary feats. However cumbersome the layers of costume, however detailed the ornamentation, the Japanese makers of this type of doll invariably achieved an effect of harmonious rhythm. The poses of the figures and the blending of colours were, like their costumes, meticulously correct in every detail before they satisfied their makers.

In their own very personal ways the English nanny doll and the Japanese figure of Shōki were designed to protect their charges. And it is perhaps not entirely coincidental that national characteristics can be seen in more than the dolls' design and costume: Nanny, very obviously a child's plaything dressed by a talented amateur, and Shōki, the untouchable ornament created by a dedicated professional, seem to typify the Western and Eastern attitude towards dolls.

Probably neither of these two characters would approve of the use of dolls in advertising, but dolls have been so used for many years. Paper dolls were an obvious choice as 'give-aways'. They have been popular both in England and the USA for nearly a century, and still feature today as cut-outs on packets of breakfast foods.

In the USA around the turn of the century, advertising ideas were far more elaborate. One, for Coats' Threads, involved five separate doll designs with additional costumes, 'supplied free of charge to purchasers of J. & P. Coats' spool cotton or crochet cotton'. The dolls themselves were something of a novelty as, by turning a disc at the back of the doll, it was possible to change the face three times.

The popularity of cut-out rag dolls was also exploited by the advertisers. In the late 1890s a printed muslin cut-out doll was designed for the North West Consolidated Milling Company, with the words 'Ceresota Flour' stamped across the shirt-front.

However, one of the most famous of all cut-out dolls was the lithographed muslin one given in exchange for packet-tops of the breakfast food 'Force'. 'Sunny Jim, Sunny Jim, 'tis Force that has been the making of him' ran the jingle, and Sunny Jim dolls were certainly the making of this successful advertising campaign. They were based on a character created by Minny Hanff, c. 1905, and were probably designed for the manufacturers of Force by W. W. Denslow. Nearly seventy years later the dolls were re-issued in England, again as cut-out rag dolls obtainable by sending off Force packet-tops; see plate 70.

The composition doll promoting Joseph Campbell's soups has also been revived, but the modern soft plastic version differs in design from the original of seventy years ago. The character is more crudely painted and in his mock Scottish outfit lacks the charm of the childish young 'Campbell Kids' which were made under licence by Horsman around 1910; see plate 70.

American firms like the Ideal Novelty and Toy Company and the Modern Toy Company produced many dolls for firms such as William Wrigley (The Spearmint Kid), and the National Biscuit Company (Uneeda Biscuit Boy), between 1914–17.

These American promotion aids were designed as play dolls, while in England the preference has usually been for the figurine. 'Johnny

Walker' of whisky fame is still going strong, as are the little golliwogs of Robertson's jams and countless others. But in modern times these old stalwarts have been joined by characters designed to be playthings, like the foam-rubber 'Mr Wimpey'.

Dolls representing real people and fictional characters have also been used to advertise films and books in the twentieth century, particularly in the USA. 'Charlie Chaplin', 'Lilian Gish' and 'Jackie Coogan' were only some of the film stars chosen, but none of these ever rivalled the popularity of 'Shirley Temple'. As herself, or in costumes representing her most famous rôles, Shirley Temple was a best-seller as a composition doll, a paper doll and in many other forms. For three years, 1934–36, the Ideal Novelty and Toy Company's Shirley Temple topped the sales in the USA. In third place in 1936 was the other best seller for many years the 'Dionne Quintuplets', made by Madame Alexander; see plate 71.

Madame Alexander was one of the four daughters of Russian parents who emigrated to New York in 1890. Three years after her marriage to Phillip Behrman in 1912, their daughter, Mildred, was born and the portrait doll of this child, made by the proud mother, started the long line of 'Madame Alexander Dolls' later produced by the Alexander Doll Company.

At first the dolls were mostly literary characters, like 'Alice', 'Little Women' and 'Snow White', but Madame Alexander also designed in 1953 a unique set of Queen Elizabeth II Coronation dolls, 36 figures in all, to add to her range of Royal and Famous People portrait dolls. But the most famous of her dolls were, without question, the Dionne Quins. Annette, Emilie, Marie, Yvonne and Cecilie were born in Canada in 1934, and the American Doll Company won the sole right to produce the genuine 'Quins' – although many firms sold five identical dolls under that title, cashing in on their immense popularity. Madame Alexander's first set represented the quins as babies, later dolls showed them as toddlers and then young children, cleverly exploiting the fame of the Dionne girls with different issues of the same idea.

Dolls with film stars' names naturally advertised their films, but doll manufacturers were occasionally inspired by more social considerations. In 1914 the American firm, Elektra Toy and Novelty Company, brought out 'Suffragina', their 'Votes for Women' doll, but sadly she was not a success.

Commemoration dolls also tend to have a limited life-span. Amy Johnson's name was on everyone's lips at the time of her historic flight, but, by the time the 'Amy Johnson' doll appeared another nine days' wonder had already absorbed the public's interest. However, portrait dolls featuring the English royal family still maintain a steady interest, whether the personage is Henry VIII or the little Princess Elizabeth. Such dolls have been produced not only in this country but also abroad: during the 1930s American, French, English and German 'Princess Elizabeth' dolls appeared, often with little or no likeness to Her Royal Highness other than blonde hair and blue eyes.

Fictional characters have also been made into dolls, often with the backing of publishing or film companies, as in the case of 'Snow White and the Seven Dwarfs'. Alice and Raggedy Ann have been issued many times as dolls on both sides of the Atlantic, while in France Bécassine books and dolls enjoyed the same popularity.

Recently, gimmick dolls for adults have been the rage, if only briefly: the Beatles and other cult figures, as well as the dolls representing the 'Magic Roundabout' characters, who have a devoted audience, of both children and adults in England as well as in France, the country of their creation. Both the USA and Russia have produced doll versions of their astronauts. It is a rather spine-chilling thought that, if spacemen dolls had been produced following H. G. Wells' books, they would have been listed as fictional characters – looking at the miniature Daleks whizzing about now one can only pray for the future of mankind.

6   *Dolls at Work:*
                     Religious

Many of the dolls in this section appear to have little or no obvious religious connections: but all either represent, were originally inspired, or were used, by priests of various religions.

Few of the Western children who have played with their amusing, gaily painted wooden or papier mâché 'tilting dolls' – which always, due to the way they are weighted, roll back into a vertical position – can have realised they were trying to knock down the image of an Eastern holy man. The ancestor of all these toys seems to have been a similarly weighted oriental figure, the Daruma.

Daruma is the Japanese name for Dharma, the revered Indian priest who brought Buddhism to Japan and then, about AD 400, moved on to China. There he founded Zen Buddhism, and spent nine years of his life in contemplation, 'during which time his legs withered away'. The Daruma doll, also known as 'stand-up-little-priest', is symbolic of the priest's endurance and will-power. Even in Japan there are many forms of Daruma, according to the area in which they are made. That of the Kansai district is of particular interest, as it is always made with blank eyes. When the doll's owner wants to make an important wish he or she will paint in one pupil, when the wish is granted the second eye's pupil will be painted in. So far my research has failed to reveal the proportion of one-eyed Daruma in Japan.

The doll illustrated in plate 72 shows a modern Japanese female Daruma – an interesting link with the Georgian English version always, but mysteriously called 'Fanny Royds' – but the more usual

Oriental and European ones are male. A Russian tilting-doll, brightly painted with his traditional balalaika, is shown in plate 9. These curious little dolls seem to have a universal appeal for they occur all over the world; and, with the exception of a few English (the Georgian Fanny Royds), American (Bouncing Billy and Betty), Russian and German examples, most seem to have an eastern and/or religious connection. 'Le noussah', as it was called in France, is invariably a Chinese mandarin and in China itself the Cantonese word for it means 'one-that-is-struck-will-not-fall'.

The religious, or at least supernatural, element appears in countries as far apart as Korea, where it was regarded as the image of an old god and called 'Or-tok-i', and Sweden, where it was known as 'Trol-ligubba' (a goblin). Even the most prosaic German parent was obliged to refer to the toy as a 'Putzelmann' (bogy man). Whatever its guise – god, priest, or historical character – it was a popular toy all over the world.

The ferocious-looking character wielding a boomerang is a straightforward representation of an Australian aborigine witch-doctor. Constructed out of wire and crêpe paper, it is one of a modern series showing the aborigines with their traditional tribal markings painted on the faces and bodies.

Many 'native' dolls have been designed in the antipodes. The Maoris of New Zealand, with their raffia skirts and feather cloaks, and usually wearing their famous tiki charms, are the ones most commonly seen. But, as most have been made in a chocolate brown plastic, they lack the ancient, wild impact somehow generated by the crude little paper aboriginal doll.

The fantastic centaur-like figure completing the trio in plate 72 is not, as might appear at first glance, a miniature English Morris hobby-horse, but is the Polish counterpart, one of the participants in the Pageant of Lajkonik (Pageant of the Little Horse). This event commemorates a fifteenth-century skirmish between the Christian boatmen of Kraków and an invading band of pagan Tartar horsemen. After the boatmen's victory they dressed themselves in the clothes of their defeated enemies and, with their leader riding the Tartar chief's horse, entered Kraków in triumph. Annually since then, a man, dressed as a Tartar chief with an imitation straw-filled battle mace in his hand and 'riding' a hobby-horse, leads an informal procession through the streets of Kraków, to the accompaniment of drums and whistles – and, no doubt, the shouts of the watching children. The brightly painted wooden 'Tartar chief', on sale during the pageant, is one of their favourite toys.

Many of the later European display and play dolls stemmed directly from the images and statues used by the Roman Catholic Church. The French went so far as to produce actual miniature rooms – or cells – as settings, suitably furnished with crucifix and prie-dieu for dolls which might be costumed in authentic replicas of the rich robes of church dignitaries, or in the plain habits of a strict order of nuns.

Carvers and turners in Central Europe made wooden figures, which might be termed the Church's Marian version of the secular Martha-like Kitchen dolls; see plate 64. Countless convent-educated girls either dressed dolls as nuns, or were given 'little sisters' correctly habited by members of the orders themselves. Behind these gifts lay the pious, if somewhat naïve, hope that the children would be unconsciously influenced for good by using these religious characters in their make-believe play.

The dolls in plate 73 show four kinds of nuns from Western, Middle and Far Eastern countries. The Kokeshi nun with a fabric veil was made in Japan. This modern doll – with a curious mixture of humility, suggested by her appropriately downcast eyes, and Parisian chic, more than emphasised by her figure – was designed, one is hardly surprised to learn, for export to France.

The other Japanese nun is unique. It was carved, many years ago, by a member of the Japanese Royal Family and presented as a gift to a visiting Englishwoman. Three years ago it was sold in aid of an animal charity, and purely by chance, I was able to discover its provenance later, when meeting the little royal kokeshi's former owner.

'Sister Mary-Ann' is a small jointed wooden doll from the Grödner Tal. Although dolls' house size, it would be rather difficult to find a suitable abode for her as she appears to be wearing the habit of an enclosed order, and so far a miniature convent has yet to be discovered. Although both she and the black-robed Kokeshi are simple wooden dolls made to represent professed nuns, the similarity ends there. As personalities, they have about as much in common as a Hollywood film nun 'extra' and a real-life Poor Clare.

The wooden Coptic patriarch and nun are modern Egyptian dolls. They display an interesting blend of ancient eastern influence in their design, and a western love of authentically garbed religious characters.

The heavenly band of angels in plate 74 came from both the northern and southern hemispheres of earth. The woven raffia wind-section was made in Ecuador. The Scandinavian straw angels have a long tradition, and have inspired many craftsmen in other northern European countries.

The use the frugal make of their local materials is always interesting. Arable farmland provided all that was needed by rural craftsmen, who used everything from dried apples and nuts to corn straw and husks to make some fascinating dolls for little or no cost. The small cymbal-basher is Czechoslovakian, a maize husk doll, a member of the mouthless family in plate 13. The tiny wax, swaddled Christ-child lying in the straw, was bought in Paris a few Christmases ago. A similar, even smaller, wax doll was also purchased, lying in a walnut shell: both are traditional French Christmastide dolls.

Although there has been a recent revival of interest in England in the art of making Corn Dollies, there remains some confusion about the exact difference between a Corn Dolly and a doll made of corn straw. As may be seen from the two illustrations of plate 74, corn dollies are not dolls at all, and have little in common with dolls made from corn except for their raw material. Why then were these plaited designs called corn dollies?

Their history is said to go back some thousands of years to a time when propitiatory fertility rites were a vital part of pagan rituals at planting and harvest times. The aid of Ceres (Demeter), the Earth Mother goddess, had to be invoked for a good crop of the vital corn, a practice which, in some form or other, was universal. In Egypt, throughout Europe and the Americas, as well as in Britain, all harvest rites involved a ritualistic cutting of the last sheaf of corn.

It was believed that the spirit of the cornfield died when the last sheaf was cut, and so that particular sheaf was fashioned into an idol, in which the spirit could rest in peace until its rebirth the following spring at the sewing of the new cornfield. This idol of the corn spirit was brought back from the field to the barn with much singing and dancing. There it was safely housed through the long winter months to guard the precious harvest. By holding a harvest feast, and giving due praise to the Earth Mother for her bounty, Ceres was propitiated, and the care of her corn spirit ensured, it was hoped, the next year's harvest.

The shape of the idol varied considerably. In some countries it was a simple plaited pillar-shape, in others a cornucopia, the horn of plenty. In Britain there are many designs, depending in which part of country they were made; some are of ancient design, while others are modern adaptations rather than variations on the original purpose of the idol. However some, notably the Somerset corn baby and those like the Scottish Carline (old woman), embody the link with Ceres and reproduction. The baby or, more often, corn maiden represents the next year's harvest and the Grandmother (Ireland), Bride (Germany), Queen or Mother (Bulgaria), the harvest already gathered.

In some places the Corn Idol (Corn Dolly) was shaped into a figure to represent the mythological Ceres herself, plate 75. This very elaborate version is unusual not only in style but in the application of lace and other fabrics to decorate its 'dress'. It shows, perhaps, the subconscious effect of European culture superimposed upon an ancient folk custom.

The term corn dolly refers to dolls traditionally made from rye and wheat straws, oat and barley straws tend to be too soft and too short for the necessary plaiting, but both are often incorporated into the tops of corn dollies because of their decorative ears.

The elaborate, decorative palm leaf figure from Bali is linked to both the corn dollies and the Kachinas of the Pueblo Indians. Like the former it is a votive doll/idol made from natural local materials, and it is similar to the latter in that after the ritual use was over, it, too, was given to a child as a protective plaything; see plate 76.

The homes of the Zuñi and Hopi tribes of the Pueblo Indians are on the sandstone plateaux of Arizona and New Mexico, but their gods, the Kachinas, dwell in the ice and snow of the high mountains. The gods' main function is control of the weather, and the Pueblo look upon them as friendly spirits, givers of all good things. Perhaps in order to emphasise this belief that the Kachinas are kindly bene-factors, there is a special Kachina who, like St Nicholas, brings gifts of dolls and bows and arrows to the children when they are good. These dolls, or ti'kus, wear masks which denote the names of the spirits they represent. The colours used for the Zuñi tribes ti'kus are basically white with brightly coloured decorative patterns, while the Hopi ti'kus are brightly ornamented in all colours. The ti'kus are made of dried cotton-wood roots, painted, and often decorated with feathers; they are exact miniature reproductions of the masked kachina spirits.

One striking difference between the ti'kus of both tribes is that, while the Hopi often made ti'kus for decoration in the home – rather as a Christian might have a statue of a saint – or more recently to sell to visitors, the Zuñi will not only refuse to sell theirs, but will hide them away from all strangers.

All adult male Pueblo Indians belong to the cult, which is divided into several *kiva*. In some of the caves which have been hollowed out of the sandstone cliffs the Indians hold their main ceremonies, chiefly during the summer months of July and August.

The Hopi and Zuñi are both agricultural tribes, and it is probably because sun, wind and rain play such vital parts in their lives that there are hundreds of Kachina spirits of the sky, water and earth. All of them are impersonated, usually in groups of thirty or forty sets, by appropriately masked Indian dancers. In their turn the dancers had replica masked ti'kus, which they gave to the initiated children after the ceremonial rituals of the dances were over. The idea has a somewhat similar parallel in the giving of a crib or Santons to Christian children at Christmas time. But the Indians believed that the dancers, as they put on the ceremonial masks assumed, for as long as they wore the masks, the characters of the spirits they represented. Such masks, therefore, were regarded as sacred.

A few punishing Kachina spirits existed, so it was important that a child learnt which Kachina the mask fitted. No doubt the ti'ku helped them to learn as they played.

The carved wooden figure behind the ti'ku does not represent another Kachina, although such figures, life size, performed a not dissimilar function in many North American tribes. It is a totem, the hereditary emblem of a tribe. Symbolically, especially in ceremonial dances, it represents the beast or bird regarded as the protector of that tribe's people; see plate 76.

The wax dolls dressed in the robes of three Jewish priests are a most unusual, if not unique, trio. They are almost certainly Pierotti dolls, and were made in England, some time during the 1860s, for John Richard Whyberd (1847–1923). He used them to illustrate his lectures on the symbolism of the Old Testament and its fulfilment in the New. Although the dolls were carried for years to and from lectures, and handled during them, they are in perfect condition without a crack or blemish. The beards, hair, eyebrows and lashes are all set, hair by hair, into the wax, and the moulding of the dolls' limbs and in particular, their heads is extremely fine.

Another portable religious item is the traditional Polish Schopa, which illustrates the New Testament. Before Christmas groups of children in Poland, as elsewhere, went carol singing. One child in the group would be chosen to carry the Schopa, or Christmas Crib. This might be little more than a paste-board box, painted and decorated to look like the stable of Bethlehem, or it could be quite an elaborate wooden setting painted in bright colours, often with a shimmering star fixed to the top.

The children chose a house, sang a carol and then knocked, asking the householder and his family to come and look at their Schopa. Although he was not, in so many words, asked to pay for its upkeep and recompense the kind little children who trudged through the snow in order that he might have the pleasure of seeing it, the message was generally understood and proper appreciation shown. The modern Polish doll in plate 78 carries a Schopa of rather elaborate design.

Cribs or crêches have a long history. Legend has it that St Francis

171

made the first one. But, although he probably did make use of one to illustrate the Christmas story – and one feels that Brother Ox and Brother Ass would have played a prominent part if he did – the custom of the crib is much older than the thirteenth century. There are references to cribs in the sermons of at least two fifth-century saints. By the fifteenth century cribs were set up at Christmas all over Italy, but it was in the region round Naples that the most elaborate were made. Later Italian cribs sometimes required a considerable space in which to display them, as the setting could include a whole miniature Bethlehem, complete, of course, with the inn and stable and all the inhabitants. In addition, a countryside scene surrounded it for the shepherds and their flock and the kings' procession, not forgetting the herald angels – usually swaying rather dangerously from wires attached to a hidden batten overhead. Some nineteenth-century Neapolitan cribs even went so far as to have mechanical effects. I remember feeling momentarily unnerved when observing, for the first time, a sleeping shepherd's chest moving rhythmically as he breathed. By the time all the sounds and movements, the baa-ing sheep, the waterfall trickling down the rocks, the sheep dogs wagging their tails at the descending angels, had been taken in, one began to feel like Gulliver.

The cribs of Central Europe were usually carved from local woods, and were sometimes painted. These were the simpler versions, with the Holy Family and an ox and an ass set in a plain stable, and one or two shepherds, angels and the three kings without. Some of the best-known cribs were made in the wood-carving regions around such centres as Oberammergau; and, of course, the craftsmen of the Grödner Tal were famous for their religious figures long before they started making little jointed wooden dolls. But the carvers of the Tyrol also made some cribs which rivalled the Neapolitan ones for elaborate presentation. In these the characters would have beautifully carved wooden or finely modelled wax heads and limbs, and they would be arranged in a natural-looking village setting – although it must be admitted that the scenery was far more reminiscent of the Tyrol than Palestine.

The Neapolitan crib-makers achieved some of their finest effects with the wonderfully expressive terracotta heads they gave their dolls. Their counterparts in Sicily were equally famous for their carved wooden-headed crib characters, mainly because of the way these dolls were dressed. Seventeenth-century Sicilian craftsmen evolved a difficult but very artistic method of applying size-soaked pieces of material to the figures, arranging the complicated draperies while the fabric was still wet and overpainting once the natural-looking robes had dried into shape. The dolls worshipping round the manger in plate 79 are Italian, of the eighteenth century. They show some of the more usual styles and media: the kneeling Madonna has a wax head, St Joseph a carved wooden one, while the King's is papier mâché.

Most of the true Santons (little saints) so popular still in France, should perhaps not be regarded as dolls, but these little pottery figures are so much part of a French Christmas that they must be mentioned; see page 179.

There are also what might be called Santon-dolls, which are genuine dolls dressed in the manner and performing the functions of the original santons; and these, of course, are entitled to their place. Originally the santons were brightly painted little figures made in Provence from the local clay, which is ideal for moulding purposes. The Provençaux still claim that only santons made from clay deserve the name, and the organisers of the famous Marseilles Fairs – 'Mecca' for Santon collectors – decreed that santons made from wood were ineligible.

Until quite recently santonniers rarely signed their work but, like the kokeshi-turners in Japan, they tended to keep to their own personal styles when making their little characters, some of which may be under 5.0 cm (2 ins) high, although others may be 60.9 to 91.4 cm (2–3 ft) tall. The smaller santons are more popular, probably because with these it is easier to achieve the aim of all santon collectors – a complete countryside scene in which to place the stable housing the Holy Family. Naturally this is the centrepiece of the setting, but there are hundreds of extras, human and animal, ranging from the village curé to the gypsy coming down from the wooded mountain-side to worship the Christ Child.

There is a traditional way of arranging the santons forming the central group, just as the Japanese have a formal position for the dolls of Okina-matsuri. To the left the villagers, with an assortment of animals and birds, and led by the curé with his red umbrella and monsieur le mayor, form one section. The shepherds, with their flock, take up their position on the right, with the fishermen coming up from the harbour in the near distance, and the wood chopper and gypsies coming down from the hills in the background. A blue- and a pink-robed angel are placed on the stable roof on Christmas Eve and, at midnight, the Christ Child is laid in the manger. The three Kings, or Wise Men, have not been forgotten. Their procession is gradually moved each day a little nearer to the village so that, by Twelfth Night, the Feast of the Epiphany on 6 January, they are grouped outside the stable with their gifts of gold, frankincense and myrrh.

Dolls were made not only to commemorate the birth of Christ, but also that of the Prophet Mahomet. The *Ariges-el-Mouled* (literally, dolls of the Birthday), in plate 80, are colourful sugar dolls, decorated with even brighter paper flowers. They are still sold from little fairground-type booths in the streets of towns all over Egypt on the feast day marking the birth of the Prophet. These dolls are usually bought for or by small girls: the boys buy, or are given, *Halowet Mousa* (literally, the sweets of Moses). These are pink sugar animals – rather similar to our Christmas sugar mice and sugar pigs – but in Egypt made to represent horses with little riders.

If the purists do not accept crib figures as dolls, it is hardly likely that they will admit decorated sugar-cones into that category. But what *is* a doll? To a child it could be 'a stick animated by love', to a primitive adult an idol to be worshipped, to the more sophisticated an object of beauty or interest to be collected and treasured.

A comprehensive history of all the dolls in the world would emerge as a set of encyclopaedias, but it is hoped that enough examples have been included in this handbook to suggest the wide range of the dollmaker's craft and the powerful attraction of the doll itself.

CAPTIONS TO ILLUSTRATIONS

A Card Game, based on F. Upton's Golliwog and Dutch dolls books, and a carved wooden 'dutch' head, see pages 20, 22

B The European 'Lilli' doll, the forerunner of the American 'Barbie'

C & D From Mrs Woollacott's family album; her Pierotti grandfather and his daughter, her mother

E Santons: modern examples of these traditional French Christmas figurines, see pages 173-4

F A page from a toy distributors catalogue, see page 54

G Tiny wooden dolls-in-eggs, pegged Victorian and modern turned Italian examples, see page 18

H Modern adaptation of the traditional Japanese Matryushka, see pages 17, 19

I A page from the Schoenhut Catalogue of 1915, see pages 32-3

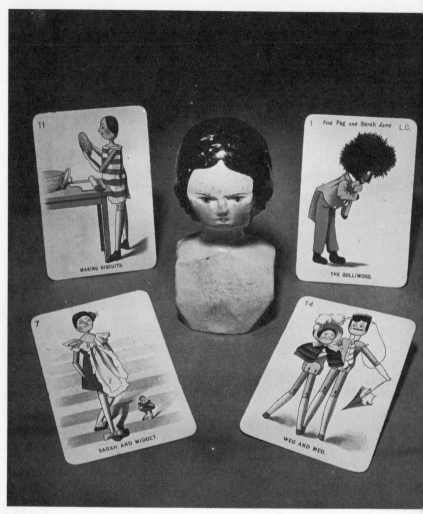

A

C

D

E

English Model Dolls, Dressed and Undressed.

11634. English Model Dolls, dressed in long robes as babies, es made to take off, size 1, 10/6; size 2, 14/; size 3, 18/; size 4, 24/; , 33/; size 6, 30/; size 7, 42/; size 8, 54/; size 9, 66/; size 10, 72/; , 100/; size 12, 110/ each.

11635. Model Dolls, wool costume, boy and girl, the pair in box ete, 4/6.

11636. Gutta Percha Dolls, dark or golden hair, dressed, 8/6, 12/6, ... 60/ per doz.

11637. Dolls' Costumes, set consisting of hat, muff, shoes, collar in wool, 9/ per doz. sets; in satinette, 8/6 and 12/ per doz. sets.

11638. Composition Dolls, imitation human hair, 2/6, 3/6, 4/, 4/9, 5/6, 7/8, 10/, 12/, 13/6, 15/, 18/, 21/, 24/ per doz.

11639. Model Composition Dolls, flowing hair, wool bodies, 7/, 8/6, ..., 14/, 16/6, 18/6, 21/, 24/, 27/, 30/, 36/ per doz.

No. 11640. English Model Dolls in fancy wool costumes, size 1, 1/6; size 2, 2/; size 3, 2/9; size 4, 4/6; size 5, 5/6; size 6, 7/6; size 7, 9/6; size 8, 10/6 each.

No. 11641. English Model Dolls, dressed in Llama costumes, size 1, 12/; size 2, 15/; size 3, 24/; size 4, 27/; size 5, 30/; size 6, 34/; size 7, 45/; size 8, 50/; size 9, 60/; size 11, 72/; size 12, 84/ per doz.

No. 11643. Dressed Rag Dolls, 3/, 4/6, 8/6, 12/, 16/, 24/, 36/, 48/, 54/ per doz.

No. 11644. Dressed Rag Dolls, short costume, 18/, 24/, 30/, 39/, 54/ per doz.

No. 11645. Dressed Exhibition Rag Dolls, long or short robes, made to take off, 4/, 6/, 8/, 9/, 10/, 12/ each.

No. 11636. Gutta Percha Dolls, glass eyes and wool bodies, 4/, 8/, 12/, 16/, 24/, 30/, 36/, 42/ per doz.

SILBER & FLEMING,

Manufacturers,

Importers, Warehousemen,

and Agents,

LONDON.

When ordering, please state the amount desired to be paid for dressing, as a small doll can be well dressed for 1/9 up to 30/ each; a medium size doll from 3/6 to 40/ each; a doll of No. 11663 size, *represented in drawing*, from 20/ each, or as shown in drawing, 60/ each, according to the quality of materials used.

No. 11663.

No. 11663. Dressed.

glish Model Dolls, with inserted hair of light golden colour. The head, arms, and legs are made of fine wax, the body is stuffed wool, and covered with fine cotton cloth, the whole doll being proportionately and properly shaped so as to fairly represent the n form. The drawing represents a doll photographed wrapped in paper, as usually supplied to the trade. This doll is made in different sizes or varieties. The smallest size, No. 11647, is 13½ inches in length; No. 11656, 22½ inches in length, and the here shown, No. 11663, is 32½ inches in length. The prices are not regulated entirely by the length of the doll, but also by size of the head. No. 11647, 1/4; No. 11648, 1/9; No. 11649, 2/; No. 11650, 3/; No. 11651, 3/6; No. 11652, 4/6; 11653, 5/6; No. 11654, 6/6; No. 11655, 7/6; No. 11656, 8/6; No. 11657, 10/6; No. 11658, 12/6; No. 11659, 15/6; 11660, 18/6; No. 11661, 21/; No. 11662, 24/; No. 11663, 30/; No. 11664, 40/; No. 11665, 50/ each.

G

H

I

INGENIOUS CONSTRUCTION OF THE *"Schoenhut Doll"*

SEE the Patent STEEL SPRING HINGES having DOUBLE SPRING TENSIONS and SWIVEL Connections.

NOTICE:—No rubber cord is used.

No more loose joints.

NEVER needs re-stringing.

NO Broken Heads.

All parts tightly held together, at the same time all joints are very flexible, and move smoothly, and will stay in any correct position placed.

All our Dolls have Wrist and Ankle Joints.

Entirely *made of wood.*

Even the *head is solid wood.*

Hands and *Feet* made of *Hardwood.*

The heads on the *"Schoenhut Dolls"* are cut out of sol wood and are painted with fine oil paints, so that they can b washed when soiled. We guarantee that the heads will n break and the paint. will not wash off. Of course, with roug usage it is possible to knock or chip the paint off, the same as o any other kind of painted wood work, no matter how fine it may be, and against such usage we cannot give a guarantee

The feet of all "Schoenhut Dolls" are made of hardwood and have two holes in the soles to receive the post of our unique Metal Stand that goes with every Doll.

The one hole is straight to hold the foot resting flat, and the other hole is oblique to hold the foot in a tip-toe position.

The shoes and stockings have two holes in the soles to correspond with those in the feet.

See illustrations above.

List of Doll Museums

Arkansas
Beaver Geuther's Mini-Museum, Beaver.

California
Anaheim Be De Armand Doll Museum, 1238 So. Beach Blvd., Anaheim. Big sign says Hobby City. Large building filled with antique dolls.
Big Bear Lake Doll House Museum, Mrs. Elsie Henderson, Box 97, Big Bear Lake.
Lomita Kuska's Doll Museum, 24301 Walnut St., Lomita. 1,200 dolls.
Los Angeles Los Angeles County Museum, Exposition Park, Santa Barbara Ave. and Hoover St., Los Angeles. 500 dolls from Shirley Temple's collection. Open free daily.
Pacific Grove Millers House of Dolls, Pacific Grove. Operated by Gina Miller.
San Bernardino Ruby Adams Peak's 800 Dolls, 1477 Lugo Ave., San Bernardino (by appointment only).
Santa Ana Charles W. Bowers Memorial Museum, 2002 N. Main St., Santa Ana.
Santa Monica Bulah Hawkin's Doll Museum, 1437 6th St., Santa Monica. 2,000 dolls in a 100-year-old English house.
Santa Rosa Mrs. Alameda Clausen's Museum, 618 Silva Ave., Santa Rosa For children, admission is one button.

Colorado
Manitow Springs Colorado International Doll Museum, Mrs. Norma Rideout, 107 So. Path, Manitow Springs.

Connecticut
Greenwich International Doll Museum, Field Point Park, Greenwich.

Florida
Homestead Mary Cole's Pink Doll House, Homestead. 100 French and Swiss mechanical dolls.

St. Petersburg Ruhamah's Doll Museum, Mrs. von Hof, 2801 Beach Blvd., So. 55th St., St. Petersburg. Open weekdays or by appointment.

Winterhaven Museum of Old Dolls and Toys, U.S. Highway 17, Winterhaven.

Illinois

Normal State University Historical Museum, lower level of Milner Library, 200 block of S. School Street, I.S.U. campus, Normal 61761.

Indiana

Bruceville Hanna Squire's Doll Museum, Bruceville, near Evansville.

Carlos Mother Goose Land Museum, Mrs. Wayne Tharp, RR 1, Carlos. 1,000 dolls.

Canton Countryside Doll Hospital and Museum-Antique Shop, Route 2, Salem. For entrance, see Mrs. Fred Elliott, four miles east of Salem on R.D. 56 at Canton.

Lafayette Doll Museum, Lafayette.

Iowa

Cedar Rapids Museum of Dollorama, Cedar Rapids.

Des Moines Mason Home Museum of Dolls, Lenore Mason, 3808 Fifth Ave., Des Moines.

Lisbon Doll Haven, Alma Pickert, Route 1, Lisbon. 300 dolls and a doll house.

Waterloo Violet Fairbanks Doll Museum, 1220 Walker St., Waterloo. Open weekends, and after 5 p.m. weekdays by appointment.

Louisiana

Lafayette Lucie's Doll Museum, 117 St. Louis St., Lafayette (by appointment only).

Massachusetts

Boston Salem Children's Museum, Essex Institute, 132 Essex St., Boston (free). Dolls and toys.

Oak Bluffs The Hansel and Gretel Doll and Toy Museum, Oak Bluffs.

Sandwich Yesteryears Museum, The Thomases, Main St., Sandwich. Dolls and doll houses.

Wenham Wenham Historical Association and Museum, Elizabeth Donoghue, Rt. 1A, Wenham. Dolls, toys, and doll houses.

Michigan
Detroit The Children's Museum, Detroit.

Nabraska
Brownville Muir House, Corner of Atlantic and 2nd St., Brownville 68321.

Palmyra The Village Doll Museum, Palmyra.

Nevada
Virginia City Way It Was Doll Museum, Virginia City.

New Hampshire
Brattleboro New Hampshire Doll and Toy Museum, 4 miles east of Brattleboro, Vermont.

New Jersey
Flemington Raggedy Ann and Andy Doll Museum, Mr. and Mrs. Bache, 171 Main St., Flemington.

New York
New York Aunt Len's Doll and Toy Museum, 6 Hamilton Terrace, N.Y. 10031.

Brooklyn Children's Museum, Brooklyn Institute of Arts and Science, 200 Eastern Parkway, N.Y. 11238.

Metropolitan Museum, Fifth Ave. and 82nd St., N.Y. 10028.

Museum of the City of New York, 1220 Fifth Ave., N.Y. 10029.

New York Historical Society, 76th St. and Central Park West, N.Y.

Rochester Strong Museum, Margaret Whitton, 700 Alans Creek Rd., Rochester (open within 4 years).

Ohio
Milan Ohio Museum, Milan.

Oregon

Jacksonville McCully House and Doll Museum, Jacksonville.

Klamath Falls Lola Chalmers Hospital and Museum, 1304 Warden Ave., Klamath Falls.

Portland Jeanette Mowery Collection, 3845 S.E. Ankeny, Portland. 3,705 dolls.

Wecoma Beach Lacy Doll Museum, Wecoma Beach. 3,000 dolls.

Pennsylvania

Douglassville Mary Merritt's Doll and Toy Museum, R.D. 2, Douglassville 19518.

Philadelphia Atwater Kent Museum, 15 S. 7th St., Philadelphia 19106. Dolls and toys.

West Chester The Chester County Historical Society, 25 N. High St., West Chester 19380.

South Dakota

Murdo Prairie Doll Museum, Murdo. Open daily in the summer.

Texas

Denton Art Department Gallery, North Texas State University, Denton 76203.

San Antonio The Doll House, on the grounds of the Witte Museum, San Antonio.

West Marshall Frank's Doll Museum, 211 W. Grand-Hwy, 80 West Marshall. Over 500 rare dolls.

Vermont

Shelburne Shelburne Museum, 7 miles south of Burlington on Rt. 7. Open daily from 9 to 5.

Washington, D.C.

Washington, D.C. Smithsonian Institution, 1000 Jefferson Dr., Washington S.W. 20560.

Wisconsin

Milwaukee Milwaukee Public Museum, Milwaukee. Historical dolls.

Bibliography

Bachmann, M. and Hausmann, C., *Dolls the Wide World Over* (Harrap, 1973)

Boehn, Max von, *Dolls and Puppets* (Branford Co., Boston, 1966)

Caiger, G., *Dolls on Display, Japan in Miniature* (Hokuseido Press, Japan, 1933)

Chapuis, A. and Draz, E., *Automata* (Neuchatel, Switzerland, 1958)

Coleman, D., E. and E., *The Collector's Encyclopedia of Dolls* (Crown Publishers Inc., New York, 1968)

The Age of Dolls (Coleman, Washington, DC, 1965)

Hillier, Mary, *Dolls and Dollmakers* (Weidenfeld and Nicolson, 1968)

Jacob, F. G. and Faurholt, E., *Dolls and Doll Houses* (C. Tuttle Co., Japan, 1967)

Lambeth, M., *The Golden Dolly, Corn Dollies through the Ages* (Cornucopia Press, 1963)

White, Gwen, *European and American Dolls* (Batsford, 1966)

Yamada, Tokubei, *Japanese Dolls* (Tourist Library, Tokyo, 1955)

Index

186

187